Keep the River Flowing

Keep the River Flowing

Facing Up to Life—Alone

by

Sylvia A. Culver

Beacon Hill Press of Kansas City
Kansas City, Missouri

Acknowledgment is made to the publishers of the following copyrighted works which are quoted briefly in this volume:

Cowman, Mrs. Charles E. *Streams in the Desert,* vol. 1, Grand Rapids: Zondervan Publishing House, 1976 reprint.

Elliot, Elisabeth. *A Slow and Certain Light.* Waco, Tex.: Word Books, 1976.

Fickett, Harold L., Jr. *James: Faith That Works.* Glendale, Calif.: Regal Books (G/L Publications), 1977.

Graham, Billy. *Angels: God's Secret Agents.* Garden City, N.Y.:Doubleday and Co., 1975.

Jones, E. Stanley. *Abundant Living.* New York: Abingdon-Cokesbury Press, 1942.

Solzhenitsyn, Alexander. *August, 1914.* New York: Farrar, Straus and Giroux, 1972.

Contents

Preface

It has been over 10 years now since a kindly surgeon stood in the hospital hallway following six hours of surgery on my husband and spoke that dreaded word, *cancer.* There followed another 15 months of illness, yet another surgery, and six extended stays in the hospital. During those days we learned the art of living one day at a time.

Near the end, we were planning to bring Weldon home, but about 5:30 one morning I received a call from the hospital that he was asking for me. I raced those 15 miles to the hospital, driving as fast as narrow Kentucky roads would allow.

When I walked into his room, I was utterly amazed. There was such a radiance in his face! His thin, pale features that had been so gaunt were transformed; his eyes shone like stars. I had never seen anything like it. He threw his arms around me with such strength and spoke those words every wife loves to hear, "You're beautiful!"

Gently teasing him, I answered, "I think your eyesight is not so good."

"No," he replied, "It is amazing how well I have been able to see all through this illness."

He spoke of the goodness of the Lord, and raised his arms as he praised God. For about a half hour he remained in that state of elation. I did not know it at the time, but that was his good-bye to me. Though we did have him home for a few hours before he went to be with the Lord, those moments we shared together that early morning will remain always in my mind and heart.

A few days earlier, Weldon had murmured to me one day from the hospital bed, "Don't worry, I'll always be by your side." As he feebly spoke that promise, I felt a sense of wonder. The very air in the hospital room seemed pervaded with prophetic mystery.

Leaving the funeral home where our many friends had gathered to comfort us, my youngest brother-in-law was escorting me back home. As we crossed the narrow street and stepped from the shade into a patch of sunlight, I was suddenly aware of another presence with us. I seemed to hear again those familiar footsteps I had heard so often. Weldon's presence was so real, I turned to look to my right side. But just as quickly, he was gone. He seemed to depart with a great bound of joy.

I had seen nothing with my 20-20 vision, but the experience was as real as if I had seen it all quite clearly. Deeply moved, and unable to speak for a time, I remembered his words, "Don't worry, I'll always be by your side." When finally I was able to speak to my brother-in-law and tell him what had happened, he replied, "That's strange; I had the same feeling."

Such a high experience is not the common stuff of everyday life. Who knows why God allows us these faint glimpses into that other world? Perhaps they are given to keep our faith burning bright through the dark days that engulf us when we go back down into the valley of daily living.

Some months later, when loving, supporting friends began to go about their normal activities and life seemed to settle down again to being "so daily," I hit bottom. Sitting at my typewriter at work one day, I felt suffocated with grief. I knew I could not type another word. Being alone in the office at the time, and scarcely realizing what I was doing, I crept into the inner office with its many shelves filled with hundreds of books.

Like a drowning person, I reached out. I grabbed a book—any book—and let it fall open. These words in bold print appeared waveringly before my tear-dimmed eyes: "Remember you are not alone—*NEVER ALONE*. At the time of seemingly greatest aloneness He is closest, watching every move on the checkerboard of life."*

What an answer! God broke through my desperate grief that day to show me the reality of His love and personal concern. Many times since then, through His acts of loving-kindness to me and my children, I have been made aware of His constant love. At times I have felt unseen spiritual forces at work on our behalf.

Somewhere during those dark days I came across these meaningful words: "Change is difficult at any age, yet all of life—from birth to death—is a process in which we must make peace with new circumstances. And no change can be more devastating than to find oneself suddenly alone, after many years of marriage." I was experiencing the "anxiety of the middle way" which Paul Tournier describes so well in *A Place for You*. I was in the situation "between letting go of a firm support and taking hold of a new one."

I soon realized I had no choice but to see things through. I must not look back. I must make peace with the tremendous changes that had come to my life. Though now I walked alone, I must learn to be a complete person and, with God's help, build a whole new life for myself.

In these pages I have sought to share the beautiful ways in which God has led along a sure path during these intervening years—and even before, preparing me for this traumatic experience. It has indeed been a shining pathway.

—Sylvia A. Culver

---

*Jones, *Abundant Living*, p. 115.

1

Keep the River Flowing

He that believeth on me, as the scripture hath said, out of his belly shall flow rivers of living water (John 7:38).

For those from the East, the seat of emotions is the belly. We of the West like to say, "I love you with all my heart," but our emotions are really felt at gut level. When upon reaching a certain age, one goes through a period of stress, he suddenly realizes that something in the abdominal area is giving trouble. Prolonged stress can wreak havoc with the entire digestive system.

Jesus is saying here that the power of the Holy Spirit will flow from the deep-down inner source of our being, and this river can flow out to bless and strengthen others. The supply of spiritual power comes from believing in Him.

And what a beautiful image He used: water—crystal-clear, life-giving water. If we are to reach out to others, and not allow the river waters to stagnate within ourselves, creating pollution and accumulating self-destructive poison, we must keep the river flowing.

When my young son stands a full 15 minutes under the hot shower, he little realizes what it's like to have a water shortage. Long before he was born, our family lived for five years in India where water was in short supply. Our water came from a deep well, laboriously drawn up with a bucket and rope, then carried two buckets at a time around the house and up the stairs to our apartment. There it was poured into those large, black earthenware jugs balanced on rope rings on the edge of the cement drain inside the house.

For our daily bath, we rationed ourselves a half bucket of water. Standing inside the cement drain, we would take a wash pan of water and soap ourselves all over. Then with a tin cup we would carefully dip water from the bucket and rinse off. Besides being scarce, our water was hard water. Using soap really produced no suds, but only a scum in the wash water. After five years of having our linens washed on a wooden scrub board with yellow soap and that hard water, our bed sheets would almost stand alone. So we learned how precious is good, soft, clean water.

Jesus promised an inexhaustible source of good water, a flowing river that need never run dry. That river can flow from its Source and through us on out to others, and in the process, we ourselves are cleansed and strengthened by its life-giving flow.

Often broken trees and other debris form a barrier for the passage of the swift-moving water. Or an accumulation forms at the bottom of the river that hinders the flow— mud and sludge. It is all hidden out of sight at the river bottom. But there are symptoms that show its presence.

There are those who look always on the dark side of life, whose days are filled with constant complaint and negative attitudes. Symptoms of mud and debris are many and varied. And like the sea animal threatened by exposure, who throws out a black, inky substance to provide an escape, such a person hides his real self behind problems and frustrations.

Some rivers roar as they make their turbulent way over obstacles in their course. There are some personalities who have an urgent need to hold center stage. What we often mistake for a display of egocentricity may be a cover-up for feelings of inferiority, or some deep-seated malaise of personality—some unresolved inner conflict of soul.

Oh, for the ability to see ourselves as others see us, or better still, as God sees us. It takes courage to take even an honest glance within, and special grace to be sufficiently objective about ourselves so that on occasion we can have a good laugh at our own expense.

Often there are barriers of prejudice or preconceived notions that stand between us and others. These, too, keep the river from flowing. Have you ever met a person for the first time and thought, "My, that's a dull one!" only to discover later what a fascinating person he really is? We need to ask God to keep our minds open and help us hold judgment at bay, so the river can continue on its way.

It is healthy, also, to remind ourselves that *not everybody is going to like us!* (Of course, that's their loss!) There are times when oil and water simply won't mix. It does not necessarily mean that one person is right and the other wrong; it simply means the mixture is not in balance. The important thing is to maintain a right attitude—not the easiest thing to do when one's emotions are upset.

For more than 30 years I have held interesting secretarial jobs for an amazing list of fascinating people—leaders, writers, mission directors, presidents of institutions. Once, some years ago, I had a boss who didn't like me—painful yet to admit. Of course, the reason he didn't like me is clear to me now. I was sitting in judgment on him; I didn't approve of the way he "kept shop." Besides this, in our work we were thoroughly mismatched. There is simply no way a mule and a race horse can pull the same plow. In such cases, it is best to recognize this fact objectively, and to mutually agree to form a separate corporation, which we did.

I learned much from that painful experience. And aren't our best lessons learned in some of our most difficult circumstances? I saw things about myself I had never seen before. I had not always done my work as "unto the Lord." How many times had I worked beyond my strength in order to hear those words, "Good job, Sylvia!" I was getting ego satisfaction from hearing all those "well dones." It's painful to sit under the "tree of enlightenment," but an excellent way to grow.

This unhappy experience also taught me something more about Christian love. Right in the middle of it, I heard Corrie ten Boom speak briefly, giving her witness on a Billy Graham TV program. Her words met my need: "You know, God is just as interested in the other person's problem as He is in yours."

So when we cross swords with another, I believe Christian love is not some mushy, emotional sentiment we call love, but rather the exercise of triumphant beneficence that rises above the conflict and says, "I wish you well."

Sometimes a problem will originate entirely with another person. Not long ago my dear friend Kate (not her name) paid us a visit. She is a widow of a minister, now teaching school in the same small community where she and her husband had pastored. One evening as we walked over the local golf course, we shared together some of the perplexities of being a new widow. She told me of her attempts at friendly conversation with members of the congregation—both men and women—as she had always done as the pastor's wife. Frequently, when conversing with some layman, his wife would quietly walk up, place her hand on the husband's arm and say, "Joe, it's time to go home." After this happened several times, she reported, it finally dawned on her what was going on. Laughing aloud, she remarked, "I finally said to myself, 'Sister, *you've* got a problem.'"

Tension may arise from a totally unexpected source. A lovely lady, very close to me, sometimes has a problem in the initial stages of forming friendships with certain women. Once they get to know her, of course, there is no barrier. Her problem is a perfect figure! She is 46 years old, has two lovely daughters, but measures 36-25-36. (I know because I sew for her.) Puzzlement about her perfect figure was so amusingly expressed by one of our Chinese workers, a close friend, who saw her for the first time in years. "It just isn't natural," he remarked, "that you still look like you did when you first came out here as a young girl. You ought to be getting a little fat and middle-aged like my wife!" Yes, even perfection can be a barrier in our relations with others.

Giant boulders may block the flow of our river—some deep sorrow, some tragedy, or a multitude of trials that crush us and block the river completely. These boulders may be so enormous that even the heaviest of machinery cannot remove them. When this happens, we need to dig a diversionary channel for our river.

It was during our early missionary days in India that God first showed me how to dig a diversionary channel. I was lying ill in the guest room of a friend whom I was visiting on another mission station. Just a short time earlier we had lost our twin babies, born too soon. My body was still weak and my mind depressed. It was easy to ask, "What is God doing to me?" Dark thoughts roamed the corridors of my mind as in a squirrel cage, spinning round and round and getting nowhere. I was weak and so smothered by depression I scarcely had the energy to keep breathing.

As I lay on that cot, I twice heard the voice of a missionary teacher who lived in a bungalow on the other side of the compound. With a note of fear in her voice, I heard her tell of the grave illness of a young girl student who lay unconscious with a high fever in their guest room.

Not realizing what brought me off my cot, I slipped out of the guest room and walked home with the missionary. Upon entering the bungalow, the two women teachers and I entered the sick room, and there lay a beautiful Indian girl, unconscious with a high fever, her long, black hair strewn over the pillow.

Those two women teachers faced an awesome responsibility. One could well imagine the consequences to their school and their work if anything happened to this young girl who had been left in their charge. Feeling a strange moving of the Spirit in my heart, I quietly said, "Let's pray." As I prayed a simple prayer for the healing of the girl, it seemed all the unshed tears of my own sorrow flowed from my heart. God's presence was very real in that room. It was none of our doing; He simply came to our aid. I sat down in a rocker in the living room to see what would happen.

Some time later, the doctor finally arrived; and the girl's fever was much reduced. I can still see the puzzled face of the older teacher as she stepped to the lamp and studied the thermometer that had earlier registered the raging temperature of the sick girl. The doctor never was able to diagnose the illness. By suppertime, the girl was sitting up in bed reading American magazines and ready for her evening meal.

As I walked back to my friend's home, I marveled at the intense joy that had been mine for a while and the relief that had come to my mind and heart. By helping me dig another channel for my river, God had brought surcease for my own sorrow. That day He showed me His plan for keeping the river flowing, even when giant boulders stand in the way.

Mrs. Charles E. Cowman (for whom I did secretarial work in 1940) had known great sorrow in her life and had triumphed over it. I knew her when she was in her mid 70s. She exuded radiance, and her lovely brown eyes fairly danced as she often shared stories of the remarkable experiences and adventures the Lord had given her. In her devotional books, which are so well known to the reading public, she shares precious messages God gave her as she walked the pathway of grief. One message of particular significance in my own life I found in *Streams in the Desert* (pp. 35-36). It reads in part:

> *This thing is from me* (1 Kings 12:24).
>
> My child, I have a message for you today; let me whisper it in your ear, that it may gild with glory any storm clouds which may arise, and smooth the rough places upon which you may have to tread. It is short, only five words, but let them sink into your inmost soul; use them for a pillow upon which to rest your weary head, THIS THING IS FROM ME. . . .
>
> Are you passing through a night of sorrow? This thing is from Me. I am the Man of Sorrows and acquainted with grief. I have let earthly comforters fail you, that by turning to Me you may obtain everlasting consolation (2 Thess. 2:16, 17).

And so, when the giant boulders of grief or pain enter our lives and threaten to block the flow of that river, it is well to remember that this very thing must first pass through the Father's permissive will before it reaches us, and like Job of old, we will "bow down and worship" our loving Heavenly Father. As we worship and adore Him, He will show us how to keep the river flowing. His great love can then be shared with His other children whom our lives will touch.

2

The Prayer of Faith

All those who pray, sooner or later come to the realization that there are different kinds of prayer. There are regular day-by-day devotional prayers, prayers of thanksgiving, prayers of praise. There are meditative prayers, as we wait quietly before God for His word to us. There are short prayers, and there are long prayers.

Gallant young mothers, burdened down with the care of small children, have learned the art of "praying on the run." There is the prayer of deep concern a Christian may occasionally feel when he senses that someone, somewhere is in need of help. A prayer for the unknown one in need is sent up to our Father who sees and knows all. At other times, the Holy Spirit expresses through us those prayers of "groaning that cannot be uttered." And there are prayers of anguish, born of deep desperation.

In my home church in the small southern Illinois town of Herrin, there was a group of praying women who often gathered to pray for a need of one among their group, or for some need in the church or community. Kneeling together in some home, or at the church altar, they shared scripture promises together. Then they began to pray simultaneously, each one immersed in her own prayer and thus set free to forget those around her. Mind, heart, and soul were focused in deep communion with the Father.

Those were old-fashioned Methodist women who knew how to reach out to God with the prayer of faith. Often their prayer sessions were fairly brief; at other times they prayed much longer. They remained on their knees until they had "prayed through," everyone present feeling the assurance that God was going to answer. They may not have known what the answer would be, but they had the assurance that their prayers had been heard in heaven. Often there were shouts of victory. I have seen elderly women in this prayer group become so blessed by the power of God that they danced around the room like young girls, their faces radiant, literally overflowing with the joy of the Holy Spirit. Some of these women have gone on to glory, but a few of them still remain in the church today as a living testimony to God's willingness to answer the prayer of faith. I have always been thankful that I had my spiritual roots in close fellowship with such women of prayer.

Alexander Solzhenitsyn, in his book *August 1914*, describes two different kinds of prayer.

> His daily morning and evening prayers, overfamiliar and mumbled in haste while his thoughts raced ahead to cope with more mundane matters, were like washing one's hands while fully dressed: a mite of cleanliness so small as to be almost imperceptible. But concentrated, dedicated prayer, prayer that was like a hunger that must be satisfied and for which there was no substitute—that kind of prayer, Samsonov recalled, always transformed and fortified him (page 316).

Prayer has the power to transform the one who prays. Moses "wist not" that his face shone after he talked face-to-face with God. When Stephen, at his death by stoning, "cried with a loud voice, Lord lay not this sin to their charge," his radiant face must have pierced the heart of young Saul at whose feet the garments were laid. Praying for someone who has wronged us can so change a heart as to turn anger to love. Perhaps this is the greatest transformation of all.

A desperate need can bring an agonizing torrent of prayer from the deep, hidden wells of the soul. I recall my first such prayer as vividly as though it were yesterday. I was only 16, having begun my Christian walk only the year before.

Ours was an estranged family. Children in such families suffer consequences that parents, involved in their own troubles, little dream of. During a domestic crisis one summer, Dad took the children (I was the eldest) and moved us to a smaller village away from the town where I had been attending high school and where my home churcn was located. In those days I had no way to travel the seven miles to school and to church.

Upon hearing of my plight, Helen, a woman of prayer who served our church as youth director for over 20 years, remarked to a mutual friend that she wished she could take me into her home for my last year of high school. But there was a problem; she would have to gain the consent of her husband.

Without telling my dad, I went ahead, by faith, and registered at the high school for my senior year. I later mentioned to my dad that there was a woman in my church willing to keep me in her home so I could go to school.

Day after day I waited for Helen to give me her final answer. Now it was Saturday night, and school was to begin on Monday. I had an appointment to meet her the next day, Sunday, to get her final answer.

It was a hot Saturday night, late in August, as I lay on a pallet on our living room floor. Through the screen door, I watched a blood-red moon creep over the horizon.

I had never seen such a moon before. Gazing at that awesome sight, I knew that my whole life hung in the balance that night. I scarcely knew how to word a prayer, but I groaned in my spirit. Dad called in once to ask if I were ill.

At that same hour my friend, Helen, was tossing and turning on her bed, wondering what to do about this skinny girl with the big, brown, pleading eyes that reminded her so much of a frightened gray mouse. My face floated before her as she tossed on her pillows. Finally, it seemed the Lord asked her, "Are you going to obey Me, or will you please man?" In desperation, she prayed, "Father, I am going to obey You, but will you please take care of my husband!"

The next morning at breakfast in her tactful way, she finally gained her husband's consent to bring this unknown 16-year-old girl into their home. I didn't learn until later that she promised she would help him several hours a week in his downtown restaurant, since now she would have a young girl at home to help relieve her of some household chores. When she made that commitment, she little realized how much training she would need to give me before I would be of any real help to her.

On Sunday afternoon Helen was late in arriving for our appointment. Dad was growing restless with waiting, and was just about to compel me to get into the car and return home when Helen came huffing and puffing around the corner of the house. It seemed by then my dad was no longer in the mood to discuss the possibility of my staying away from home. But Helen began to talk to him.

The Holy Spirit put words in her mouth, for she really knew very little of our family circumstances. She pleaded with my dad to allow me a chance to finish high school where I had been previously enrolled. She stressed the importance of an education for my future. Then softly she reminded him that it was sin that had caused the trouble in his family.

My dad turned pale as Helen pleaded with him, and being under deep conviction, was anxious to get away quickly. So he hurriedly agreed that I could come to her home the next day. What joy was mine!

The next day Dad took me to Helen's house, which I had never seen. As I stepped up on the porch, a shaggy old dog came barking from the kitchen to greet me. Taking one look at me, he seemed to say, "Oh, it's you!" and turning around quietly went back to his slumber on the kitchen floor. Such was my welcome to my new home for the next three years. The following spring, before I graduated from high school, Helen fell very ill. I remained on to help the family through the summer months, and no mention was made of my returning to my own home.

Since her husband was in the restaurant business and did not get home until around midnight, Helen and I had many long evening hours to share together. As she told of her experiences in faith and prayer, I grew in spiritual understanding. My whole personality changed. She often told me emphatically, "You are just as good as anyone!" How her joyous love pulled me out of a teenager's feelings of inferiority and set my feet on a wonderful new path. Love and peaceful surroundings did their healing work in both body and soul.

When I try to imagine what my life would have been without God's direct intervention in answer to that Saturday night of desperate prayer, a cold chill settles over me. Truly, all the rest of my life did depend on that fateful decision.

Sometimes a prayer of faith brings a price with it. An elderly woman in my hometown, whom I have known for many years, told me this story: In her younger days she married a handsome young coal miner who had just returned from the battlefields of France after World War I. Apparently he had picked up the gambling habit while serving in the army. As the years went by, he gambled more and more. The habit had such a grip on him, that she did well at times to keep food on the table. For years she prayed about this heavy burden in their family life. Being a true Christian, she did not nag her husband, but went more and more to prayer.

Finally, after a number of years, their financial situation was such that she prayed a prayer of desperation: "Lord, do anything! I am willing to pay any price, only cure my husband of the gambling habit that is destroying our family."

Some time later as they sat on the front porch, he saw an acquaintance passing across the street and asked her who it was. She knew it was a friend and was astonished that he didn't recognize the person across the street. In that way, they discovered his eyesight was failing.

For several months her husband stayed in the Veterans Hospital in St. Louis, during which time there was no family income at all. Those were the darkest years of the Depression, and she had four people depending on her for food—her own son, and a sister-in-law, whose husband was away searching for work, with her child.

My friend was able to find a temporary, part-time job as a clerk in a local store at a salary of $2.50 per week. Each Sunday she put in her 25 cents tithe offering at church, and trusted God to provide. Within a short time, she found a better job with a photographer and was able in this way to support the household of four people during the many months her husband was hospitalized.

When her husband was finally able to come home, he went into business for himself. With the aid of a magnifying glass, he was able to take care of his business accounts, but in all the years to follow, he was never able to see well enough to gamble again. To some, this may seem a strange answer, but these are the facts as she related them to me.

The prayer of faith will bring salvation to a soul. For many years during the Depression, Helen often sent food to help a family that had fallen on hard times. The older son would come to the screen door and quietly let their needs be known. She would go to her cupboard and prepare a sack of food for them. The father of the family, Otto, never seemed to be able to make a go of it. They knew many years of poverty and distress.

In later years, when I was home on furlough from the mission field enjoying a visit with Helen, this same son, now a grown man, came to her screen door. But this time he was requesting prayer for his father who lay in the hospital unconscious, gravely ill with acute appendicitis.

Helen went to get her prayer partner, Flo, and they went out to the prayer room located in the small mission south of town. A group of men from our church were sitting in the hospital room with Otto. In the middle of her prayer, Helen got specific and asked God to allow Otto "to come to his right mind" long enough so the men could lead him to the Lord. The two women continued to pray until they felt God had given the answer.

They later learned that their prayers were answered. Otto did regain consciousness, and the men around his bed led him to Christ. He gave a clear witness of salvation before he died, his face filled with a radiant joy. One can only marvel at the celebration that must have taken place in heaven as the angels rejoiced over Otto's coming into the Kingdom that night.

In later years when the circumstances of that family improved, and Helen had been widowed, they often invited her to their home on holidays to share their family meals.

Abraham's servant, who had gone back home to Abraham's country to find a wife for his master's son, Isaac, stood by a well in prayer. He asked God to send out a young maiden who would not only give him water, but who would also volunteer to water the camels. Even before he was finished with his prayer, the beautiful Rebekah stood before him and gave him water, and his camels also. Truly, God delights in answering the specific prayers of His believing children. "All things, whatsoever ye shall ask in prayer, believing, ye shall receive" (Matt. 21:22).

God may at times give a prophetic vision in answer to the prayer of faith. Weldon and I were ready to leave for California shortly after our marriage, and we knelt in Helen's dining room to have a farewell prayer. I who had never been more than 300 miles from home was setting out on a long journey with my new husband. As we prayed, she later told us, God gave her a vision of our future years together—"a long journey," she said, "with many high mountains and deep valleys. The journey seemed to go in a great circle and return again to the place of its beginning."

Now as I look back over the 29 years that were given us, that is exactly how it was. We met in Wilmore, Ky., where I was a summer student at Asbury College. Often during our sweetheart days, we walked to a small railway bridge near a cemetery where many old saints are buried. The following year we were married.

There were many high mountain peaks and some low valleys in our lives together. During his final illness, Weldon remarked one day, "Well, some of your life with me has been very hard, but you can say one thing, it has never been dull!"

It was July 4, 1938, when we realized it was God's plan for us to be together. Exactly 30 years later on July 4, 1968, he was buried in the same small cemetery near the bridge where we had talked of our youthful dreams.

Some time after my husband's passing, my married children discovered in his baby book, so carefully prepared by his mother more than a half century earlier, her written statement that on July 4, 1914, Weldon as a newborn babe was carried out into the sunshine for his first outing. Three July 4ths—all so significant. Truly our times are in His hands!

Our long journey had taken us up hill and down hill, and we had arrived back at the same spot where our love had its beginnings. Helen's vision, given to her in prayer, was fulfilled in every detail.

At one time or another, all of us have known the prayer of faith that brings victory during a time of battle with the forces of evil. These conflicts take place on all sorts of battlefields and for all manner of reasons.

Years ago, I learned the secret of letting God fight my battles for me—it saves a lot of wear and tear. Our part is to draw near to Him in prayer, continuing to watch as we pray and obeying His smallest instruction—then *victory is ours!* Often during a crisis, we have no idea what the solution will be. But when God fights our battles for us, He fights to win. Often the outcome is not only glorious, it is downright startling. I have seen strenge things happen in answer to prayer when waiting on God to help find a solution to a seemingly insoluble problem.

When our Lord entered the fiery furnace with the three Hebrew children, not a hair of their heads was singed, and there was no smell of smoke on their garments. So God can bring us through great trials, not only unharmed, but actually strengthened and blessed by the outcome of the battle.

Defeat can be turned into victory because of the prayer of faith. Occasionally in life, calamity may fall upon us from nowhere, without warning, as it did on Job.

Before we fully realize what is happening, we are inundated in some terrible calamity.

Dale Carnegie once wrote that when we have faced the worst life can do to us, we have nothing left to fear. Great testing need not leave us quaking in fear. We can rise above, stronger than before, but this comes as a process worked out in our lives on a day-by-day basis, as we learn to keep our hearts open to Him.

Like an oyster, we may take great pain and turn it into a thing of shining beauty. Friends may wonder at the glow on our faces, little dreaming of what might have brought about this special illumination from within. After all, it is His pleasure to educate us, and while this process is going on, He continually surrounds us with His abounding love.

All of God's servants are undergoing a period of training, I believe, in preparation for a very important assignment in the world to come. God is getting us ready for something beyond—something that even our keenest imagination cannot envision. If we allow Him to do His work in us while passing through this school of life, and if we refuse to grow bitter or complaining when the battle gets fierce, we will then be ready for whatever task He has for us.

3

The Prayer for Healing

Since my early Sunday school days I have believed that God can heal our bodies in answer to prayer. I have, in fact, been the recipient of divine healing on more than one occasion. I have seen God answer a prayer for healing even when lofted heavenward by one who at the time did not confess to follow Him.

Just a few years ago, during a hospital experience, my elderly mother shared an incident with me that she had never told me until that day.

The year I was 10, we lived in a dreary mining camp in southern Illinois. How can I forget the drab sameness of the "company" houses and the cinder sidewalks! We children counted houses as we ran home from school, to make sure we entered "our house." To this day, when I drive through a housing area where all the houses are built alike, I still feel the sense of depression and futility I knew as a child.

Our only heat in the drafy four-room house was a coal stove in the living room. During that cold, hard winter I was stricken with double-lobar pneumonia. As I lay unconscious with raging fever and labored breathing, the young doctor held out little hope for my recovery. (Those were the days before antibiotics.) As my mother shared this story, she told of how she cared for me in my illness until she reached the end of her strength. Sinking exhausted into bed one night, she prayed: "God, don't take my daughter. If You will spare her, You can use her in far-off lands." When my mother prayed that prayer, I doubt that she had ever heard the word "missionary."

As I sat in the hospital room listening to my mother recount this story and reflected on the years of missionary service my husband and I had shared, both in India and Taiwan, I marveled at God's answer to the cry of a young mother in such desperate need. Laughing aloud, I said, "Well, Mother, God really answered your prayer, didn't He?" As she recalled those early memories, she smilingly agreed.

Before my husband and I were ever to reach the mission field, however, there was to be yet another healing miracle for me. In 1942 we were serving two small Methodist churches down in the river country of southern Illinois. Since I was having some difficulty with a wisdom tooth, we went to see a dental surgeon in Cairo, Ill.

Upon checking me over, he discovered what he thought was a benign cyst in the roof of my mouth, a small protrusion about the size of the tip of my small finger. I had not even been aware of the time when the growth had developed. A few days later, the surgeon performed a simple excision, using only local anaesthetic. During the operation, Weldon noticed a troubled expression on the doctor's face. For several days I lived on liquids while waiting for the stitching to heal.

After some days we returned to the doctor and with a serious look on his face, he presented us with the lab report from St. Louis. The word "carcinoma" was on the neatly typed report. I was only 25, the mother of a small son. The doctor urged us to go to St. Louis for X-ray treatments, the cost of which would exceed our annual salary. As I lay in bed that night, I wondered what we should do. Fear walked with me during those days.

One day we decided to drive north to Herrin, my home to pay a visit with Helen and Flo, two prayer partners. We asked them to pray for my healing. They anointed me with oil, and we had a victorious season of prayer. They shared many scripture promises with us relating to our future ministry.

My confidence had increased, but still I was not quite sure in my own soul about the outcome. Several days later, the women of our little country church held a missionary meeting in one of the homes of our small village. The hostess had taken little scripture promises from a small box and placed one on each tray, along with our refreshments. Each guest read her promise aloud.

I picked up my card and read aloud: "Fear not, for I am with thee" (Gen. 26:24), "And there shall be no more curse" (Rev. 22:3). As I read, I felt a gentle shock of electric-like power go through my whole body from the top of my head to my feet. From that moment I never doubted that God had healed me. The seal of our faith was the birth of our second son that next fall—a child of promise.

The X-ray treatments were never taken. It has now been 34 years since that healing, and I have never had a recurrence of the problem. God kept His promises given to our two praying friends. We later served three terms on the mission field. "Hath he said, and shall he not do it?" (Num. 23:19).

Helen and Flo, our two praying friends, have had many unusual answers to prayer for healing and for other needs in our small town. When those two get together to pray, their combined faith is invincible. They know all about "moving mountains"!

On one of our furloughs home from the mission field,

Weldon and I had an interesting conversation with Harry Stone, also a member of our Herrin church.

Brother Stone had established a small mission in the south part of town. He had a prayer room behind the meeting hall where he kept a fire going in winter so people could come and pray at any hour. As he stood in that prayer room, he told us this story:

Some months earlier he had fallen gravely ill and lay unconscious in his home. It appeared he would not survive. Some women from our church, Helen and Flo among them, came to his home to pray for his healing. Placing their hands gently on his head, they prayed simultaneously, as was their custom. During that season of prayer, Brother Stone paid a visit to heaven.

"The Lord did not permit me to see anything," he said. "But I heard a conversation between the Father and the Son." Weeping great tears of joy in remembering the experience, he said, "Weldon and Sylvia, I have never heard a voice so gentle and kind as the voice of the Son."

It seems the Father and the Son were discussing Brother Stone's case. One of them mentioned that "a petition has come up." The other replied, "But the reception committee is all ready to greet Brother Stone."

The Son turned to Brother Harry and gently asked, "Are you willing to go back?" Brother Stone answered, "I don't want to leave this wonderful place and return, but if it means I can bring others here, then I will go." And so he was spared a few more years to carry on his ministry of witnessing and praying. I am sure that when he finally did return to that wonderful place, the welcome committee was all ready again to receive him with open arms.

While living in the capital city of Taipei, Taiwan, where our mission had its headquarters, we had a Chinese driver who took all of us in the mission truck to our various meetings and classes. Four missionary families shared the use of one truck. Our driver was a soft-spoken, gentle Taiwanese named Tsing ti-Hsiung. I had just learned that his only son was seriously ill. I knew only a few words of Chinese and he knew only a little English, but somehow we managed to communicate. I asked about his little son. A look of great sadness came across his face as he replied, *"Mei yo pan fa"*—there is no hope.

His utter sadness pierced my heart—I understood well his deep grief and sense of impending loss. We had had a similar loss in our own family.

Immediately upon returning home, I said to my husband, "We've got to do something for Tsing ti-Hsiung's baby!" Weldon hurriedly called our wonderful red-headed physician, Donald Dale.

The grandparents of the baby, being Buddhist, were very reluctant to allow the child to enter a Christian hospital. But since it was apparent the child was dying, they finally gave their consent.

The babe was taken to the Seventh Day Adventist hospital down the street from our mission compound. After giving what treatment he could, Dr. Dale felt that if the child could survive the next 48 hours, there might be some hope. The German nurse later told me with tears that she had never seen a little body so badly dehydrated. When she pressed his flesh, it remained indented for lack of fluid.

As soon as the child was in the hospital, I had gone to my room to pray. It was only a short prayer—"Lord, if You can get glory to Your name, will You heal this child." My burden soon lifted and I felt God would answer our prayers. The child lived!

More than 10 years later when we were living in Kentucky, a letter came one day from Tsing ti-Hsiung, written for him by a friend who could write English. Inside the letter was a photograph of his family, with a small arrow penned above the head of a handsome young lad. "This is the boy for whom you prayed," he wrote. And now the proud father was sending us his thanks by post across the Pacific. It was our God who answered prayer and healed that desperately ill baby, and it was His name that received the praise and glory.

The miraculous healing of my brother-in-law, Norman Cook, stands out in my mind as one of the most remarkable I have ever witnessed.

A native of Warsaw, Ind., Norman married my husband's only sister, following a four-year courtship. Some say that marriage is really made on earth, not in heaven. But their great love for each other is such that I have often thought they really must have had some help from heaven. One reason their happiness has been kept so alive, I believe, is that they have freely shared it with others. Through the years, they have never sought to "bottle up" their joys for themselves, but in their home have provided hospitality and companionship for hundreds of friends and strangers.

At an early age, Norman and Muriel went out to Taiwan to help lay the foundations for a missionary work on that Island. Serving as field director, he spent the long, hot summers traveling and playing with the Venture for Victory basketball teams that came out from the States to tour the Orient.

Norman's rugged body vibrated with strength and energy, and his mind was just as active as he delved into many books. His enthusiasm for life was contagious.

When his work took him far from home for long weeks at a time, his greatest delight was to arrive home in Taipei a day ahead of schedule. Even if he reached the compound at 2 a.m., he never entered the gate quietly, but leaping over the top of the high wall surrounding the compound, he would shout with his great, booming, husky voice: *"Where's my wife?"* All of us knew when Norman came home.

On September 1, 1966, following a strenuous summer with the basketball team, Norman fell ill. Dr. Ward Bullock, then serving with the Naval Area Medical Research Unit, Taiwan, was called in for consultation with the missionary doctors. "Japanese B-type encephalitis," was the diagnosis.

For 10 days, Norman lay unconscious in the hospital with three young men of different missions taking turns around the clock to stay by his side. The prognosis was gloomy indeed. At the beginning it was felt he might have a 30 percent chance of living. Then suddenly, the prognosis was death. "There is no use to pray; this man will die!" the doctor affirmed.

But missionaries and Chinese Christians throughout the island went to prayer. A group of three men, one a missionary doctor, slipped into the hospital room one night and anointed him with oil and prayed. Some of our Chinese workers were given assurance of his healing.

News of Norman's illness reached the Winona Lake Free Methodist Church where his brothers and sisters attended. During the Sunday morning worship service, the pastor prayed for Norman Cook, gravely ill in Taiwan. When the pastor finished praying and looked up, Norman's brother, Bob, was standing at the altar. "Pastor Reid," he blurted, "I don't know if my brother is alive or not, but I know if I ever want to see him in heaven, I've got to get right with God. Please help me!" He fell to his knees and began to confess his sins.

Pastor Reid then turned to the congregation. "We want to focus intercessory prayer for Norm's healing. But God cannot hear prayer if there is sin in the heart. If any of you have known sin, then come, kneel, confess, get right with God, then we will go to prayer as a church."

Twenty-seven people lined the altar that morning. Each sought divine forgiveness. Then the entire church went to prayer. No further hymns were sung, the choir anthem was forgotten, the offering and morning message were laid aside. The church as a body went to "effectual, fervent prayer." They prayed right through the lunch hour and on until 2:30 in the afternoon. Then God gave a united sense of peace. The whole congregation sensed it. They "knew" Norman was going to get well.

After a week had passed, the doctors in Taiwan began to realize Norman might survive after all. But then came an even worse prognosis: "Even if he lives, his brain is so damaged he will never know his wife and children. He will never work again. Perhaps after a year, he might be able to dress himself. Don't even pray that he will live." Following those awful words, Muriel wrote of her battle as follows:

> The struggle inside of me was beyond description! I wanted Norman to live more than I have ever wanted anything. I realized I loved him much more than my own life. I was sick at my stomach with fear. The predicted brain damage held even more terror than death. God gave me the verse in John 11:40 where Jesus said, "Said I not unto thee, that, if thou wouldest believe, thou shouldest see the glory of God?" I knew this meant I had to relinquish Norman totally over to God, even if it meant brain damage, or God would not be glorified.
>
> I was so afraid of losing my husband and of blocking God with a wrong attitude that I got on my face on the floor and cut every tie I had ever had with Norman. He was my childhood sweetheart, the answer to my dreams, all I ever wanted as a husband, the father of my children, my joy and future. I relinquished all to God to do as He wanted so that we would not miss the glory of God. Then peace came.

Although my instructions were just to trust God and He would do what was right, I never knew whether He would heal Norman until the day he regained consciousness.

Dr. Dick Hillis, director of Overseas Crusades, hurriedly caught a plane from the States for Taiwan, fully expecting to preach Norman's funeral. As he headed for the hospital, he was troubled at the thought of facing Muriel. Climbing the hospital steps, he begged God for help.

Until that moment, he had forgotten a note that his wife, Margaret, had handed him for Muriel. Reaching in his pocket, he pulled out the note to give her. It contained the same verse given to Muriel by a friend from southern Taiwan—John 11:40: "Said I not unto thee, that, if thou wouldest believe, thou shouldest see the glory of God?" Neither he nor Margaret could have dreamed that the same verse was given to Muriel from two different sources, separated by 8,000 miles. Those words came straight from God, reminding Muriel to trust Him. Whatever He wanted to do would be best—would be perfect. God did see fit to restore him to health.

After Norman regained consciousness and was able to talk to us, he related how late one afternoon, while drifting in and out of sleep, he suddenly saw a long, wide staircase rising into the air from the foot of his bed. Dad Culver (who died in 1954) was standing at the top—bald head, moustache, a big smile—his arms opened and with both hands beckoning Norman to come. "I began to move up," Norman said, "exhilarated and relaxed. Then I thought, What about Muriel and the girls? I turned my head to locate them and the vision vanished. A euphoric peace flooded my soul. All fear was gone."

Muriel wrote of her own experience, amazingly similar to Norman's:

Norm and I were together in the dark, looking up at some huge boulders straight above us. Suddenly without a word he began to bound up over the rocks toward a great light. His body was vibrant and full of great expectancy. Although no words were spoken and my feet were firmly planted on the ground, I knew Norman was going to meet Jesus! Because we have always had such unity of spirit, I was instantly filled with the same joy he had, even though he was leaving me. Then the vision was gone.

During the time of Norman's sickness and recovery, five missionaries or missionary children of our acquaintance in the Far East died. On Taiwan, two members of the same family met death. Three of the five deaths were from encephalitis.

After Norman had regained consciousness, doctors checked his coordination and mental capacity. One of them asked him to subtract from 100 by 7s. Norman remembers thinking to himself, "He's nuts! I can't even do that when I am well." But he accomplished the feat.

Following 10 days of unconsciousness, Norman found himself totally weak, a prisoner in his hospital bed, unable to sit up or to feed himself. For one who had all his life been so physically vigorous and active, such total incapacity was frightening indeed. In his helplessness, he became very fearful for his family and for himself. He wondered what he would do in the event of an earthquake.

"In my total helplessness," Norman wrote, "I turned everything—everyone over to God. For the first time in my life *total trust* took over. Again, peace, victorious peace, filled my being."

During the succeeding two years, Norman gradually regained complete physical strength and has continued as rigorous a schedule as he did in former years. All of us who know and love him, marvel at God's mighty healing power, even in the face of such dreadful predictions made by a team of physicians. Man's extremity proved once again to be God's opportunity!

Some believe that God wills wholeness for every man. Yet it is obvious that He does not grant healing to every person for whom we pray. Then comes the big WHY?

Elisabeth Elliot gives what I believe to be a good answer to this troublesome question in her book *A Slow and Certain Light*:

> He did not make all deaf men hear, or all blind men see. He got Paul and Silas out of prison, but he left John the Baptist in prison—left him there, in fact, until his head was chopped off. . . . He keeps us from diseases at times and at other times lets us get them. When he lets us get them he sometimes heals us and sometimes lets us die. But in whatever he does in the course of our lives, he gives us, through the experience, some power to help others (pp. 65-66).

If our faith in a sovereign God is secure, and sickness still persists after we have prayed and have met all the conditions known to us, then we can only bow to our all-wise Father. We know He is a God of love and that He is no respector of persons. Therefore it would not be in His character to willy-nilly grant healing to some and non-healing to others. Could there be some deep meaning that we have not yet fathomed in the words, "Neither are your ways my ways saith the Lord" (Isa. 55:8)?

Is there something in the scheme of things yet hidden from us? "Now we see through a glass darkly" (1 Cor. 13:12). God certainly has a plan for each of us and a work for us to do. Whether that work is to be done in this world or the next, we are to await the summons of our loving Father who sees all things from the end to the beginning, and who does all things well.

4

Sit Still, My Daughter

*Then said she, Sit still, my daughter, until thou
know how the matter will fall: for the man will
not be at rest, until he have finished the thing
this day* (Ruth 3:18).

In those ancient words spoken to Ruth, her daughter-
in-law, Naomi revealed a faith that was willing to wait.
When we have already done all that we can, there comes a
time to wait on God to make the next move. Naomi was
confident that God was at work. And as is often the case,
down in the unseen future much more depended on that
fateful decision than was realized by the persons then
involved in the drama. Ruth was to be a member of the
ancestral lineage of the coming Messiah!

When during a crisis of decision every fiber of our being cries out to make some move—to take some action—
it takes a special kind of discipline to sit still and wait on
God. One of my fascinating friends has often remarked,
"I'm the kind of person that likes to have 'all my ducks
in a row,' but all my life God has been teaching me to
wait on Him."

In our Western culture, where a young man and a

young woman choose each other for marriage, rather than the family being involved in the selection, a grave responsibility is placed on young and untried shoulders. At a very young age I sensed that I was totally inadequate to come to such an important decision on my own; I knew that God would have to guide me very clearly in the matter of marriage.

On a starry night, the summer I was 14, I was sitting on a broken-down car seat in the backyard of my grandfather's southern Illinois farm. All the family had gone to bed. Out in the country there are no city lights to dim the stars, and on that night I had a glorious view of the heavens above me.

As I gazed spellbound into the star-filled sky, the multitude of heavenly bodies seemed to float and move gently above me; I felt at one with the universe. My mind reached out to the future with youthful vision and wonder. A strange feeling came over me that someday I would travel around the world. And mingled with my dreams was the thought that the young man I would someday marry was far away on that night. It was true. On the night of my star-filled dreams, he whom I would later marry was a schoolboy in Foochow, China.

As the years passed, there were many "signposts" that eventually led me to him. The summer I approached my 17th birthday, we had an old-fashioned revival meeting in a brush arbor in the south part of our town. The evangelist came from Wilmore, Ky., and frequently in his sermons he made reference to Asbury College—the first of many of my "signposts" to come.

At an altar service one evening, I joined a group of women to pray for one of my young friends who was having personal problems and really needed God to take control of her life. The idea of anything unusual happening to me was far from my mind. I covered my face with my handkerchief as I prayed, and the women around me prayed simultaneously as they interceded on behalf of needy souls.

Suddenly, a shining light seemed to surround me. A message came through to me—whether by words, or by impression I do not know. But the message was that God had chosen a young man I was to marry and we were to do a work together for Him. (It was not until a year later, when standing in our home church one Sunday, that the Lord told me the work was to be on the mission field.)

This was my very first experience where God seemed to talk directly to me and for days afterward I pondered in my heart the meaning of all the Lord had revealed to me. I shared my experience only with my friend Helen.

When talking together one day, Helen remarked that if God had such a plan for my life, then I must go to college. There was no money at all for school but she took me to the nearby teacher's college (now Southern Illinois University) to register for the fall quarter. I had only 50c to my name.

We had heard that the college had a Federal Student Aid program (one of Roosevelt's bootstrap operations to help pull the country out of the Depression). I made application for an FSA job, although my prospects of getting such work looked very dim. There were more than a thousand applications for perhaps 150 jobs. Within a few weeks, however, I received a postal card advising me that I had been assigned one of the jobs, working two hours a day for the head of the art department. My salary would be $15.00 a month, enough to pay my tuition. Room and board were provided from other sources. In this way I was able to complete two years of college, take practice teaching, and qualify for an elementary teacher's certificate.

In September, 1937, I was able to secure a teaching post in my hometown, teaching the same grades and subjects I had worked with in practice teaching. I earned the magnificent salary of $85.00 a month during the two years I taught, but how exciting to have my first job!

As the years went by, I continued to ponder in my heart about the vision God had given me. I kept looking for that "young man" that was to come into my life.

On New Year's morning, 1938, I had a strange dream. The young man of my vision walked in Helen's front door, sat down in her large red chair, arose from the chair, smiled at me and backed out the door. I guess it was God's way of telling me, "This is the year."

To maintain my teaching credentials, I had to attend college each summer. As that first summer approached, I sent away for various college catalogues. I had always wanted to go to Asbury College, but felt it best to save my money and wait and go there when I could stay for a full school year.

I thought it might be fun to go to Colorado that first summer. I had never seen the mountains. In fact, I had never been more than 300 miles from home.

One day in conversation at the table, while listening to my excited plans about going west for summer school, Helen remarked, "Yes, Satan would like to get you off on a detour." It was so unlike her to make such a remark, that I puzzled over it for several days.

As I crossed the main street of our town a few days later, the Lord spoke to me directly: "Sylvia, you are to go to Asbury College this summer." That settled it. No more dreams of going west. I had only six weeks to get ready for summer school.

In those years, young women wore hats to church on Sunday. As a young woman, Helen had sold hats in the local department store. She took me to buy a new hat. As we walked in, she spied a large leghorn hat with a floppy brim, a narrow band of black velvet ribbon around the crown, and a cluster of daisies on the front. The price was downright sinful, I thought—$8.00. She placed the hat on my head, stood back looking at me admiringly, and prophetically exclaimed, "That hat will get your man!" Little did either of us realize the truth of her prophecy as we laughed uproariously together.

Summer school began with an excited flurry of registration and classes. As I looked over the students in the dining room, I sensed right away that the young man of my dreams was not there. I wrote to Helen: "He is not here. They are either too young or too old." I felt foolish and blue.

One night in the dorm I had a talk with the Lord. I had spent four years dreaming about a "big romance," and had seen no results. I wondered if the whole thing was a figment of my imagination. As I prayed, I told the Lord I was weary of my foolishness, and if He didn't bring the matter to pass until I was 40, it was all right with me. But I asked Him to please remove the foolish dreams from my thinking. I was going to settle down and study and make top grades in my courses. The whole matter was surrendered to Him.

Unknown to me, the young man of my dreams, while not a student at the college that summer, was living in the village of Wilmore. He sang in the church choir. On that first Sunday he had seen a strange girl with a big hat sitting in the back of the church. He wondered who she was. He knew the girls on either side of her, but this stranger in the big hat really caught his eye. On the way home from church he made some rather startling remarks to his mother, as he raved on. As all mothers will, she cautioned him to be very careful until he found out more about me.

He was working on the college tennis courts that summer and had seen me playing tennis with my roommate. But for some strange reason he felt unusually shy.

He did not even know my name but referred to me as "brown eyes."

Finally, one evening he got up enough courage to share his feelings with Bill, a quartet buddy. As he described me, Bill and his wife realized my identity. As Weldon talked on, they both exclaimed, "Oh, you mean Sylvia Furlow!" Thus for the first time, he heard my name.

It was arranged, then, that I would be invited to go with Weldon to the forthcoming picnic which the quartet had planned for July 5. But before that first official date came about, we had two conversations together.

I was sitting up in my room studying for a history exam when a note was delivered to me from Weldon, who was waiting downstairs in the parlor:

I don't know you, and you don't know me, but there's nothing like getting acquainted. . . .

So down I went to the parlor to meet him for the first time. After accepting his invitation to go with him on the July 5 picnic, we shared a quiet conversation together, sitting side-by-side on a sofa in the parlor of the girls' dorm.

The next evening, July 4, as I peeked out the small window above the stairway of the dorm, I saw him walking around the college semicircle toward the girls' dorm. I went downstairs on an "errand" and met him there in the parlor. He invited me to go with him to the local drugstore for a coke. As we sat close together at the narrow table facing each other, and as I took a good look into his blue eyes, suddenly I knew this was the face of the young man God had described to me four years earlier. I became uneasy and frightened, scarcely believing my turbulent emotions. Mentioning that I had a headache, I cut short our conversation that evening and hurried upstairs.

It so happened that my roommate was entertaining

her mother, and so I slept in an empty room that night, on a narrow iron cot. All night I tossed and turned, comparing Weldon to what God had revealed to me four years ago. Yes, he was planning to be a missionary. And on and on, until finally the dawn's sunrays reflected from the glass transom over the door of my room. God whispered, "Sylvia, where are your doubts?" "Lord, I have none," I replied. From that moment, I was sure Weldon was the one God had chosen for me.

And during all the years that were to follow, when we settled down to the "nitty gritty"—the realities of two such extremely different personalities making a home together under one roof—it was the knowledge that God had been our "matchmaker" that gave us the steady anchor that held our marriage firm. As years passed, and we sailed through some inevitable stormy seas during our mutual process of maturing together and raising a family, it was the realization that He had planned it all, that provided the cement that bound us ever closer together. Only thus were we able to survive those rough seas as we passed from one stage of maturity to the next.

And after 30 years, on that other July 4, when we stood by his graveside, and that chapter in my life had now come to an end, it was with serenity and gratitude that my soul cried out, "Thank You, Lord, for these 30 years—for all of them!"

5

All Your Needs

My God shall supply all your needs according to his riches in glory by Christ Jesus (Phil. 4:19).

For 29 years, my husband and I shared remarkable adventures as we watched God supply our needs from day to day. Sometimes this supply came in normal, quiet ways; at other times needs were met in extraordinary ways.

It all began the morning after our wedding which was held in my home church in southern Illinois on a June night in 1939. We were married during the latter part of the Great Depression and we had about $25.00 between us after wedding costs were met. Jobs were awaiting us in Los Angeles, but we had no way to get there. As the days passed, we wondered how we could make the journey.

After enjoying a waffle breakfast at Tony's Place the morning following the wedding, we decided for some reason to go by the local post office to see if Weldon had any mail. An airmail letter from a California pastor was waiting for him. The pastor had just purchased a new Chevrolet from the factory in Flint, Mich., and he asked if Weldon would be willing to pick up the car in Flint and bring it out to California. A check for $50.00 was enclosed to cover our travel expenses. We not only had a brand-new car for our honeymoon trip to California, but all travel expenses were fully paid as well!

That was the beginning of a remarkable story of God's provision for all our needs, as we shared our years together.

When our first son was born the following year, we received through the mail a number of gifts from friends which enabled us to meet our doctor and hospital bills.

I believe our faith that God would supply all our needs had its roots in our practice of tithing. Even when Weldon pastored two small country churches and our salary was only $20 a week, the first tenth went into the offering plate. All through our missionary years, we continued to tithe our modest salary.

In later years, after we returned to the States, we heard Ford Philpot, the evangelist, mention in a camp meeting sermon that Christians ought to tithe their gross salary, not just the net salary. As missionaries, we had never dealt with gross and net. It hadn't occurred to us since coming home, to tithe our gross salary. We had always tithed what came to our hands. That evening we agreed that we ought to tithe our gross salary, which we began to do when our next check came. Within just a few weeks, our salary was raised, and the increase more than covered the amount of additional giving. I have often heard people say, "You can't outgive God," and we experienced this in our own family.

It was New Year's Day, 1952, when the Lord gave us a verse of scripture:

The land whither ye go to possess it is a land of hills and valleys and drinketh water of the rain of heaven: a land which the Lord thy God careth for: the eyes of the Lord are always upon it, from the beginning of the year even unto the end of the year (Deut. 11:11-12).

That scripture verse was the first inkling we had that God was leading us into a new direction that would some 15 months later take us to the beautiful island of Taiwan. What a remarkable picture of that island is portrayed in those verses from Deuteronomy.

But before we would arrive on that beautiful, green isle to begin two terms of missionary service among the wonderful Chinese people, there were many needs to be supplied and many adventures of faith to be realized.

When we first went out to Taiwan, we served with an organization that operated completely by faith. The mission organization under which we later served was not incorporated until our second year on the field. During that first year of deputation travel there was no salary; we were completely on our own. We not only had to secure our own speaking engagements, but had to maintain our family of four, pay the rent, buy the food, and keep the old car going from our offerings given us at missionary meetings. We had to raise enough pledges of support to provide our family income for five years on the field. Besides that, we had to secure enough cash (above our living expenses) to pay our way out to the field and return. What an undertaking! But we believed that when God calls, He provides.

It was very difficult to arrange speaking dates that first summer, for many pastors were away on vacation. Clearly what we needed was a small nest egg to get us going.

Driving one day to a speaking engagement in Indiana, we prayed aloud in the car, as was our custom. When it came my turn to pray, suddenly in the middle of my prayer, without any forethought at all, the words, "O Lord, give us a thousand dollars!" burst from my lips. I was a bit stunned by my own prayer. But my faith took hold.

As we went to our appointment, we had a wonderful

weekend of ministry at the church. The people stuffed money into our pockets as we greeted them at the church door after the service. The accumulated gifts amounted to something over $200—a good offering; but I was still expecting that thousand dollars for which I had prayed.

We drove back to my home in southern Illinois and every time the phone rang or someone knocked at the door, I jumped. I was expecting the miracle gift! Finally on the third day, a phone call came from our pastor up in Winona Lake, Ind. "Weldon, remember that little church in Michigan where you had a meeting not long ago? Well, there is a widow up there who has something for you. I think you'd better drive up there right away." Weldon drove through the night to reach the town.

When he arrived at the small town, he went to the young pastor's home, and they went together out to a farm where the widow lived. For many years her husband, not a Christian, had worked hard and saved his money. He did not trust the banks so had stashed away all his savings in a hole in the wall of their house. The wife, a devout Christian, was never able to give to the church. After his death, she went to the hole in the wall and found $10,000 that he had put away. Now at last she had a tithe gift to present to the Lord.

She called her young pastor and expressed a desire to give the money to missions. She felt it unwise to give it to the small church, fearing other members would think they need not give. "Brother Culver keeps coming to my mind," she told the pastor. He agreed that if she felt this leading, it would be a good thing to give the tithe to the Culvers for their missionary work. So on the day Weldon and the pastor went out to her home, she took out an envelope containing $1,000 in fresh bills! The three of them knelt for prayer and how she rejoiced that at last she had a gift to give the Lord. I believe she was even happier than we.

God taught us something through that gift. He often supplies our needs from the least likely source, from the least likely person, *so the glory will be His!* It would have been very easy for the wealthy widow with whom we stayed in Miami to donate such a gift. But instead, God gave it to us from a poor widow, a member of the smallest church where Weldon had a meeting—the least likely place—the least likely person! God has His surprises.

As we did our final packing and made preparations to leave for Taiwan in the Spring of 1953, there was still $400 lacking in our transportation fund. On Sunday night, the last night before our departure, our home church took up an offering for us. The total came to $470—"running over."

The next morning as we pulled into Chicago, the officer of our sponsoring group in charge of outgoing missionaries, met our train. Upon learning that all our travel needs had been met, I can still hear his "Hallelujah!" as he walked alongside the train. Passers-by probably wondered what crackpot had been turned loose, but those who know the joy of depending on God and having Him come through at the eleventh hour, can understand such unbounded praise.

In later years we were to receive another gift of $1,000 —this time totally unexpected. It was during our first year home after our last term on the field. A letter came from a lawyer one day stating that we had inherited a gift of $1,000 which would be coming at a later date when the will was probated. Really puzzled, I wondered, "What's happening now?" But two years later when we purchased the only home we were ever to own, we had our down-payment through this unexpected gift, given before it was needed.

Perhaps the most amazing story of all is how God provided for us during those last few years before my husband's terminal illness. As I look back over that span of six years before his death, I marvel at the number of unusual decisions that were made in relation to a change of job, and other business decisions that were later to affect our lives so remarkably. "The steps of a good man are ordered by the Lord" (Ps. 37:23).

In 1962, following our return from Taiwan, we realized that Weldon's health would no longer permit him to return to the intensive village and mountain evangelism in which he had engaged for the past nine years on the field. He recognized also that he was not cut out for a desk job.

The following year, he was led in a very unexpected way to accept a totally different kind of job as salesman for a Christian publishing house. His job would be to travel up and down the eastern states, selling books and music to Christian bookstores. I was very perplexed when he made such a strange decision. I did not understand what God was doing. But I remember saying to him, "I don't understand it, but I am with you." We moved to the small Kentucky college town of Wilmore, the home of Asbury College and Asbury Theological Seminary, where a number of our friends lived. I found employment at the seminary, and Weldon traveled all the way from Bangor, Me., to Miami, Fla., up and down the country selling for the publishing house.

As the years went by, he began to experience some physical difficulties, and later developed a terminal illness. The details of how God supplied all of our needs during the 15 months of his illness make an amazing story.

When we first returned to the States in 1962, we did not have any furniture, nor did we have a dollar in savings. God had for 23 years supplied all our needs, as He had promised, but there was nothing left over. But by the time Weldon's final illness came, we had medical insurance, salary insurance, mortgage insurance—all that we needed to cover us through two major surgeries and several long hospitalizations. During his illness, we often sat in our living room and talked of the amazing way God had provided for us. Had Weldon been in business for himself all those years we spent on the field, we would not have been better covered than we now were. We lacked nothing.

When I think of the staggering cost of his long illness, and realize what a burden this might have placed on my shoulders after his passing, I stand in awe at God's special love and care for us through the years.

But in order to receive such provision, we had to be willing to enter strange and unexpected doors. Like Abraham (Genesis 12) we had to go out "not knowing." It is very easy to look back and be grateful for the way God has led us in the past, but quite a different thing when we face a new move, a new decision, and are acting on faith, totally in the dark as to what God is doing.

For more than eight years now God has continued His faithful supply for my son and me. The miracles He wrought to help me complete my own college training are described in another chapter. Then came the need for our youngest son's college expenses, above what he would be able to earn in summer work.

Upon returning to Kentucky in 1972, following my two years at Southern Illinois University, I was able to purchase a comfortable home where we lived while Leland completed high school. When it came time for him to enter college, I knew I could no longer carry the mortgage. After owning the house only three years, and with the sudden rise in real estate values, I was able to sell the house for sufficient profit to cover all my son's college expenses. On my own, I would never have had the business sense to make such a good profit on an investment.

I have also experienced God's continuous day-by-day

supply of needs. An exciting account of such is noted in my diary for March 3, 1975:

A DAY OF MIRACLES! About a week ago, I was talking with Judi (my daughter-in-law) on the phone, and I mentioned that I would love to go out to Portland this summer to see my new grandson, Joshua, but I simply didn't have the money. After a silence, Judi challenged me: "Mother, I think you ought to ask the Lord for the money to come."

That night as I went to bed, imagine my amazement when I opened *Daily Light* and read, "Ye have not because ye ask not." I shut the book and prayed, "All right, Lord, I am asking you for the money to go to Portland this summer to see my children and my new grandson." I really didn't think much more about it, but this day (March 3) a whole series of miracles happened:

1. Early this morning a friend called saying someone had given her $50 to help a student, and she wanted to apply this gift to help buy a new pair of glasses for my son.

2. At lunchtime there was a letter from a certain missionary organization with cottages to rent in the East where I had hoped to spend my summer vacation: "We regret that we have no space available."

3. At one o'clock I went by the bank to pick up my federal and state tax returns that were prepared by a business friend. (I had delayed several days in picking these up.) When he told me that I would be getting more than $800 in refund, I nearly fell off my chair. MORE THAN ENOUGH TO GO TO PORTLAND! Abundant—pressed down—running over.

And so I could tell on and on the miracles God has performed through the years to supply our needs. He has kept His promise to me; my Maker has been a husband to me. As I move to the future and contemplate retirement years, I am free of fear. I know He has a plan for me and that as long as I live, my needs will be met. God never starts something He does not finish.

6

Think on These Things

Whatsoever things are true . . . honest . . . just . . . pure . . . lovely, whatsoever things are of good report; if there be any virture and if there be any praise, think on these things (Phil. 4:8).

When life got too much for Scarlett O'Hara, heroine of Margaret Mitchell's *Gone with the Wind,* she turned to the divide-and-conquer tactic: "I'll think about that to-morrow." But the apostle Paul has given to Christians a system of "displacement"—filling the mind with these great "whatsoevers," so that the terrible realities of life may be faced and conquered.

The older I grow, the more I am convinced that happiness is what we think about, and control of the mind is perhaps one of the most difficult of all disciplines, There is no remedy for the mind as powerful as that of giving thanks.

I did not realize it then, but at the age of 14, I had my first experience with this system of displacement, so well outlined by the apostle. It happened at Christmastime. Because of the Great Depression, we in that small southern

54

Illinois mining camp never knew abundance, and that particular Christmas was especially black—there were to be no gifts at all.

The day before Christmas I awoke and ran to the window to discover a deep snow had fallen in the night. The world outside was transformed. A white, glistening fairyland appeared before my delighted eyes. Suddenly I thought of my Aunt Augusta and Uncle Ben out on the farm. She was my mother's older half sister, and had always taken the place of grandmother in our family. There was always good food to be had at her house and much talk and laughter. I loved to open her pantry and sniff the aromas of sauerkraut, black-eyed peas, corn bread, and cherry pie.

As I looked out the window on that snowy morning, I had an irresistible urge to spend Christmas with my aunt. There was only one way to get there—by foot, five miles through deep snow. I dressed as warmly as I could and set out immediately. Hiking five miles through deep, crunching snow and breathing deeply of the sharp winter air was exhilarating. Aunt Augusta and Uncle Ben were all alone that Christmas, all of their children had married and were gone from home. They welcomed me with open arms.

Late that afternoon I tramped across the field, climbed through a tangled fence, and slipped into a little country graveyard no longer in use. I cut down a small evergreen tree and brought it to the house. We made colored-paper chains and popped corn and threaded it on string to decorate our tree. As twilight came on, we lit the oil lamps, and admiring the tree, sat comfortably in our rocking chairs, our feet propped on the chrome apron of the blazing pot-bellied stove. We talked and laughed, ate hot buttered popcorn, and told stories. We shared our love and dispelled our loneliness with laughter. We had no gifts to exchange, but we gave of ourselves. That Christmas when we had no gifts turned out to be the happiest of my childhood.

More than 30 years later when I visited my aunt who was then 89 and bedridden with her final illness, we talked together of many things. Suddenly her old, wrinkled face lit up with the most delighted look as she asked, "Do you remember that Christmas?" How could I ever forget it! We talked of the tree we had decorated those many years ago and of the joyful time we had shared together.

I had another special friend who daily practiced the discipline of thinking happy thoughts and doing useful things in order to escape the prison house of her pain-wracked body. We called her Pearlie. She always shared a happy laugh, and had some bright comment to make on the events of the day. Often she wrote amusing poems which she shared with us. For more than 20 years she suffered great pain with crippling arthritis that twisted her once beautiful face and body. But through all those years there continued to be laughter, good food, fun games, and reading material in that house. I always loved to visit Pearlie and play word games with her.

On our last furlough home from Taiwan, I walked over to the little frame house to tell Pearlie good-bye. As I entered the kitchen, she sat in her rocking chair and looked up at me. In that instant, both of us knew it was our final good-bye on this earth. I thought for a moment I would break into tears of grief. But suddenly, as I looked at that once lovely face, now twisted and bloated by both her illness and the medicines used to control it, the thought came to me, "Pearlie, the next time I see you, you will be beautiful." That glorious thought instantly and completely lifted my grief, and we were able to share in a happy conversation, as I told her good-bye for the last time. Some months later, after we had returned to Taiwan, I learned that she quietly went to be with the Lord while sitting at the kitchen table reading a letter from her son in California.

Then there was the time during our early missionary days when I was seriously ill. I suffered both with physical illness and with heavy mental depression.

Daytime hours were spent in the Word, poring over those great chapters in the Book of Isaiah. There were times of prayer. Strength was found for the daytime hours, but as evening approached and the body grew weaker, it seemed that all the forces of evil floated into my room, seeking to destroy me. Never before or since have I waged such a battle. Too weak to pray, I picked up an old hymnbook and, beginning at page one, feebly sang all the hymns I knew. I think there is one thing Satan dreads more than a praying Christian; it is a singing Christian. Relief came as I sang those old songs. I believe I understand why Paul and Silas sang in the prison at midnight. There was a strange power at work that night in the earthquake and in the salvation of sinners—a power that comes only from praise.

Perhaps the most difficult of all mental and spiritual disciplines is when we experience the loss of a life companion. After a long illness, my husband passed away about 3:20 in the morning, his mother and I by his bedside. By four o'clock the pastor and other friends were seated with me at the kitchen table. While the undertaker and his assistant were carrying out my beloved's body on a stretcher, those of us around the table were sharing together the many things we had to be thankful for, and how God had provided for us and had sustained us through the past 15 months of Weldon's illness. We were learning to see things from God's perspective. As we shared together, a quiet peace came to me, and I was able to get through that most dreaded of all days.

The day of the funeral, July 4, turned out to be a glorious, clear, cool day. As our family sat in the limousine, waiting to go to the cemetery, we thanked the Lord for such good weather.

As our family slowly marched down the long aisle of the church behind the coffin, a strange sense of triumph and glory surrounded me. Part of my emotions were strangely not unlike those I felt going down the church aisle as a young bride 29 years before. My eldest son remarked that he distinctly felt the presence of angels in the high balcony at the back of the church.

But it was the graveside service I dreaded most of all. When our pastor, David Seamands, began reading the Scripture lesson beside the open grave, a bird in a tree overhead burst forth with the most glorious song I think I have ever heard. It was as though nature itself was trying to tell me that this was a time to rejoice, not a time for sadness. My beloved was now in a better world, free of the pain and sickness that had for so long imprisoned him. A person in grief must be on the lookout for such messages from God. He has much to say to us, but we must have our "receiving sets" ready to hear Him.

Then there follows the need for mental discipline to rebuild one's life as a widow, to find a way to become a whole person again and to find meaning and purpose in life, even though it is now to be lived alone.

Some widows are filled with fear of business and financial problems. These matters were of no real concern to me, since I had always maintained a keen interest in business matters and in budgeting. But one of my most difficult areas of adjustment was at the social level. It had always been my husband who had launched us into new friendships. I was more shy and had simply followed in his trail, thoroughly enjoying all the friends he made for us.

Attending my first social event as a widow was an

ordeal. It was a large potluck supper. Before entering that dining room, I little dreamed how drastically life had changed for me. But I sensed it the minute I walked through the door. I was ill at ease. I didn't know where to sit—with whom I should talk. It may have been my raw sensitivity, but it seemed to me that the eyes of one or two of the women were directed toward me in a different way than I had been aware of before. This distressed and puzzled me. You see, I had entered the world of the "singles" and I didn't like it—not at all! All those 29 years, totally unaware of it, I had been sheltered with a mantle of security and protection. I had found "my place" and now had lost it. I was struggling to regain solid footing.

Katie F. Wiebe, in her article "Can a Widow Survive in Today's Church?" (*Eternity*, Sept., 1972, p. 20) describes so well some of the painful adjustments a widow faces socially, even in the church. "One of the most pressing needs of any normal person is simply to share with another adult," she writes. She goes on to tell how at various church suppers she was ushered to the table filled with children and other single women. There was no opportunity to enter into conversation with the "couples" society. "I appreciate the people, especially the men, who consider me a person worth talking to and who still has something to offer life," she explained.

During my own early months of widowhood, I attended a faculty-staff retreat. As I went to the first meal in the dining room, I didn't know where to sit. All my adult life I had enjoyed the conversation of our men friends, even more than the women, for men tend to talk more in the world of ideas. But that day, somehow, I didn't feel free to join my "couples" friends at their tables happily buzzing away in interesting conversation. Miserably, I sat at the table where the single women had gathered. I shall never forget the senior professor who took his wife by the arm and brought her to our table to join us in happy conversation throughout the meal. To this day, that act of thoughtful kindness stands out in my mind.

It was some time later, at the wedding reception of the daughter of a dear friend, that I learned a secret that was to change my feelings about social events and my part in them. The bride's mother had asked me to fill a place of honor at the reception—to cut the cake and serve it to the guests.

As the wedding guests arrived at the doorway, I braced myself with a paper-stiff smile. Suddenly my mind left the scene before me and took a long journey all the way back to India.

I saw again the little village Hindu widow with her shaved head, her precious jewelry stripped from her, dressed in a white, cotton sari. (White is the color of mourning in the East.) That little widow would never be permitted to attend a wedding in her village, even for a member of her own family. Being a widow, she would be looked on as "bad luck."

As I looked around at my many friends, at the flowers and vines gaily decorating the hallway, at my new colorful dress that custom did not forbid me to wear, at my place of honor, I thought, *Jesus did this for me!* My heart was filled with such an intense joy I could scarcely contain it. I no longer felt self-conscious and miserable. My smile was genuine. What a wonderful time I had. From that time on, my awkwardness in crowds began to diminish.

In later years, I could laugh heartily when I heard a beautiful black entertainer, Della Reese, say tartly to Merv Griffin on his TV talk show: "Merv, I've been single 16 years—and it ain't all bad!" But there was to come considerable growth before such a remark would sound amusing.

Then there were the lonely nights when the house was

filled with eerie silence and there was no quiet voice to whisper, "I love you. Good night!" Haunting memories floated before me in the half darkness of my room.

There were memories of my husband's long bout with suffering, of the look on his face when he gazed lovingly at our 11-year-old son, knowing that he would soon be leaving us. I recalled the February before he died, when he bought a lovely, warm overcoat. He stood looking at himself in the mirror, and asked "What if . . .?" and never completed the sentence. Scenes from the past—both happy and sad—floated out of my "memory banks" to haunt me and keep sleep away.

Then I began to practice "displacement"—a deliberate act of blotting out such memories with words of thanksgiving for present blessings. Often I would whisper my thoughts aloud in the darkness of my room to keep my concentration from wavering. Wriggling my toes under the clean sheets, I would thank God for a warm bed with clean, nice-smelling covers. My memory banks called up the unforgettable street scenes in Calcutta where half-naked, starving beggars lay side by side at night, like so many corpses, their stark, bony feet projecting from beneath rags and gunny sacks covering them as they groaned in troubled sleep.

On nights when the soft rain fell, I thanked God for a good roof, for a warm, dry house, I reflected on how God had miraculously given us our youngest son late in life. I recalled how we feared he would come too soon, as had his older twin brothers whom we had buried in India. I thought of the women's prayer meeting held on our mission compound, and how after those prayers, my premature labor had stopped as suddenly as it had begun. I remembered how I had carried this child a little longer, giving him more time to grow, and how finally, he was safely delivered by Caesarian section in the eighth month.

I reflected on this healthy, happy child who had come to bless our later years and how, through this divine providence, I still had "family" at home with me for a while yet. As I rejoiced in all these things, I fell into a peaceful sleep. Healing of memories began with thanksgiving.

During the first year of my widowhood, I made plans for trips to visit relatives and friends, far and near. I always tried to keep at least one trip planned ahead on the calendar. I had been driving only a few months. (It takes great courage to learn to drive when you are 50.) That first winter, my son and I made long trips, even over ice and snow, to visit friends. God protected us. My "backseat driver" had fits one early morning when mother turned the wrong way into a one-way street against rush-hour traffic in downtown Indianapolis. A flood of cars came bearing down on us with horns blowing.

Then came the trauma of our first Christmas alone. Of course our second son and his wife would be with us. But as I gazed at the rocking chair in our living room—my husband's last Christmas gift, given so grandmother could rock the visiting grandchildren—I wondered, "How will I ever get through this first Christmas without him?"

A few days before Christmas I got an unexpected telephone call. A strangely accented voice said over the wire, "Mrs. Culver, this is Colonel Chang. Remember me? I was your English student in Taiwan!" He was taking special military training in Leavenworth, Kans., and was seeking some American home where he could spend Christmas. During the eight years I taught English Reading at the Chinese Officers' Language School in Taipei, perhaps 900 different officers had passed through my classes. But remember him, I did! He had such an infectious sense of humor. It had been 14 years since he sat in my class, yet I recognized him the moment he stepped off the bus. So God sent us a Chinese guest all the way from Taiwan to make the first Christmas very special. And in His own loving way, He helped divert my thinking from that which I had lost to that which I had gained.

Jesus said, "Lo I am with you always." He is with us in all circumstances. He stands ready to come to our aid, if we will but open our eyes and swing wide the door of our hearts to receive what He has to offer us.

7

Mother Goes to College

If the Lord would make windows in heaven, might this thing be? (2 Kings 7:2).

As I continued to work my way through the maze of grief during the second year following my husband's passing, a growing restlessness began to stir within me. I began to question, "What am I going to do with my life?" An older friend said to me one day, "Sylvia, when you become a widow, you have to make a whole new life for yourself."

Early one spring morning as a wet, sticky snow fell, I tramped the golf course, umbrella overhead, talking with the Father. The words of my friend, "make a whole new life for yourself," repeated themselves in my mind like a refrain.

Long talks were held with my son, John, and his wife, exploring future possibilities. In the mid-30s I had attended a small teachers' college in southern Illinois which had now grown to a large university. After my second year was completed in 1937, I had taken a teacher's certificate and taught in a local elementary school, but had never been able to complete my college work. The longing to return to school had always been with me, but such hope seemed like a distant mirage.

During the latter years we served on Taiwan, I was enrolled with some G.I.s and American civilians in extension courses offered by the University of Maryland in a night school located near our mission compound. There were classes in government, speech, and Chinese. How exciting, after so many years, to be involved once again in the world of academics! The class lectures were discussed at our dining table. Members of the family often joked, "Mother will finish college by the time she reaches 50."

And now I found myself a widow, approaching my 52nd birthday. Not only that, I realized I would not be able to maintain our home and educate our son on my current salary. It had been necessary to dip into savings to keep our household going. I must somehow prepare myself to earn a higher salary. But so many problems stood in the way of my going to college. The very thought of stepping out on such a bold program of self-improvement caused me to quake with fear. God would have to perform several miracles to make my dream come true.

Being a habitual list maker, I wrote down the needed miracles and shared them with my children. One important item on the list was that I needed to be admitted to the university as an Illinois resident, in order to qualify for the lower tuition rate. My son, Jon, who had had some difficulty with out-of-state tuition upon enrolling in a Kentucky college, said, "Mother, it will never happen. You must not count on it." But it did happen. I was able to fulfill the 90-day residence requirement and meet certain other rulings before being enrolled at Southern Illinois University that fall. (Just a year later, the university increased the residence requirement to a full year.) Eventually, we saw all of those listed miracles granted, one by one, and *always on time!*

While still undergoing the decision-making process of returning to school, I read one day in *Daily Light* for December 20: "'If the Lord would make windows in heaven, might this thing be?' (2 Kings 7:2). 'Have faith in God' (Mark 11:22). 'Without faith it is impossible to please God' (Hebrews 11:6). 'With God all things are possible' (Matthew 19:26)."

For many years now, during a decision-making process, God has come through with a word for me. I have often had to wait for His word, but He has never failed me in the matter of guidance. And if no word comes, it simply means "Wait—sit still."

I stood that day in my bedroom looking at our family picture—my husband and I, and our three sons. Because of the late coming of our youngest son, the five of us had lived together under one roof a rather short time. As I gazed at the family portrait and considered all the problems facing me, it seemed I could almost hear my husband's voice saying: "You can do it! You can do it!" Somehow in that moment, courage came.

From that day, I began to take the necessary steps to fulfill my dream of completing my education. Of course there would come moments of uncertainty and fear. But again E. Stanley Jones's *Abundant Living* provided a message:

Relax in His Presence. Christ—the Man who met everything we meet and more, and didn't worry. Fasten your attention on Him; for it is a law of the mind that whatever gets your attention, gets you. If your worries get your attention they will get you. If Christ gets your attention He will get you. . . . Then take the next step: *Relax in His presence.* . . . Often fear and worry keep the motor running even after you are parked. . . . Let God replace the false energy of fear and worry with the true energy of faith working through love (p. 76).

As the time approached for school to begin, we were settled in my hometown some 17 miles from the university. I felt my home church and home environment was a more suitable place for my young son. I drove the 17 miles to school each day to meet my classes.

My niece, a recent graduate of the university, helped me through the confusing maze of registration. What changes had come in the registration process since my early years in college! We are now in the computer age.

Because of my years of secretarial work, it was decided that I should major in secondary education and take a Bachelor of Science degree in business teacher education.

One of the required courses for this degree was accounting. I was very nervous about that particular course; it had been nearly 40 years since I had studied math. The first day in class I was feeling pretty shaky. I heard two young fellows behind me talking under their breath. One of them said, "I'll bet she's every bit of 60!" I was so amused, I laughed within myself and forgot my fears. I dug into the hard grind of daily, disciplined study and came through the course with a passing grade.

The students at the university were really very courteous and the professors showed a kindly interest, but I found a different world than I had known there in the 30s. I was caught up in a whirlwind of class schedules along with a student body of some 25,000 energetic youth. Often I had to rush across that huge campus, and climb three flights of stairs to meet my next class. But strength was given. There was considerable culture shock, too, especially when one day a buxom, braless young woman came bouncing out of the cafeteria with something printed across the front of her T-shirt that might not pass the censors!

I was astonished and saddened one day to see a group of Hare Krishna students in saffron robes, their bald heads and topknots bobbing, as they clanged brass cymbals and chanted Eastern tunes. Their chanting was a very poor imitation of tunes I had heard many times in India.

I found that many changes had been made in the courses offered in business and office practice. Shorthand theory had to be completely relearned. I had come many a mile since first learning to type on the old upright Underwood manual typewriters. Now we whizzed away easily on electric typewriters. It was no small satisfaction for me to be listed as top of the class in the speed tests given in our advanced typing class.

I managed to survive seven quarters of school through ice of winter and heat of summer, and came through with a high grade average. I wasn't such a rusty old grandmother, after all.

On June 9, 1972 (our wedding anniversary), I marched down the long aisle to receive my diploma, along with hundreds of other graduates. There were so many graduating that two separate ceremonies were held, and having our names called out would have been unthinkable! But my mother and another dear friend sat in the bleachers with the parents. What a joy to achieve such a goal after 35 years.

During those two years of intense study, I found emotional healing. God had surely wiped away my tears and bound up my wounds.

As the spring of my final college year drew to a close, I wondered, "What next?" I had hoped to return to the mission field and perhaps teach in an American school for our support. I made application for a teaching position at the American School in Singapore. But that door remained closed. Numerous applications were sent to schools in the States. No response. All doors closed.

Finally, just two months before I had to know which road to take, a long-distance phone call came from a friend back home in Kentucky. I was being offered a secretarial job. My son was overjoyed at the thought of returning home to his old friends. It was not what I had expected or longed for, but, as Harold L. Fickett, Jr., puts it in *James: Faith that Works:*

> Anyone who places himself under the control of Christ will be satisfied with whatever station in life he has. He will realize that this is both the place and the circumstances which the Lord has assigned him. Thus he will be free from complaining, grumbling and feeling sorry for himself (p. 116).

Or, as Paul Tournier says in *The Person Reborn:*

> Faith consists in believing that where we now are is where God wills us to be; that He requires us to give ourselves wholeheartedly to the task that faces us now, and that He will surely lead us elsewhere if ever He wishes to do so. Having a mission means doing what we are doing in a missionary spirit (p. 187).

And so today as I perform my secretarial duties, I occasionally glance at my college diploma which I have framed and hung on the wall of my walnut-paneled office. The Bachelor of Science degree inscribed on the diploma may not appear so exciting to those professors who have spent a lifetime of study, but my heart sings as I think of how God, in fulfillment of a lifelong dream, made it possible for this grandmother to go to college.

8

Building Bridges

Dr. Frank C. Laubach in *Open Windows, Swinging Doors*

On the great domed ceiling of the Sistine Chapel in Rome, appears one of the great paintings of all times—Michalengelo's giant portrayal of the Creation. Suspended above, one can see the mighty arm of the Creator reaching across, like a bridge, to the creature, man, so perfectly formed of the dust of the earth, his body complete in every detail. Yet, one thing is lacking—life itself.

Building the first bridge between himself and man, the Creator reaches out to Adam whom He has made in His own image. "God is love," the Scriptures say. From that great heart of love pulsed the life-giving force, and Adam became a living soul. Thus the Creator himself became the first bridge builder.

And because God loved us so much, He later sent

70

Jesus, His only Son, who came to earth and taught us much more about bridge building. "Whosoever shall give to drink . . . shall in no wise lose his reward," He said (Matt. 10:42). "Inasmuch as ye have done it unto one of the least of these my brethren, ye have done it unto me" (Matt. 25:40). "He that findeth his life shall lose it: and he that loseth his life for my sake shall find it" (Matt. 10: 39). Thus He taught us to give of ourselves and learn to build bridges between ourselves and others over which His great love can flow, healing wounds and bringing fulfillment of human need.

Bridge building is a two-sided coin. Of all those who suffer grief over the loss of a companion, the saddest is the person who had not yet learned to build bridges.

I have seen women devote their entire lives to husband and children, sharing in work and family life with joyous intensity, and yet they failed somehow to reach out to neighbors and friends. Finally, they are left alone, children married and gone and husband now deceased. There is only one way out of such loneliness—learn to build new bridges.

It was not easy for me to reach out and form new friendships, for I was basically shy. My husband had always made new friends for us. But now I was a widow and on my own.

One day while discussing the possibility of returning to Illinois to college, my wise daughter-in-law said, "Mother, you need to remove yourself for a while from this small, religious community. You need to get out into the 'real world' and learn to form friendships with other kinds of people."

When, at the age of 52, I made the move back home to Illinois to enroll in college, I began to see that God had other things in mind for me than an education. He was going to teach me how to relate to others in the community.

In the low-rent housing area where we lived, there were neighbors who needed someone to care, someone with whom they could share their problems. At the same time, I needed to learn how to relate to them in a personal way.

One of my neighbors was Kathy, who lived with her mother just across the lawn from us. She was only 19, a tall, statuesque girl—a lovely blonde. When she styled her long hair in a certain way, she reminded me of pictures I had seen of a Russian princess.

Kathy had a rare blood disease and was kept alive with blood-thinning drugs. As a result of blood clots, she had already lost one leg, amputated near the hip. But she had come to terms with her eventual death.

Occasionally Kathy would fall ill. Hearing she was confined to bed, I slipped over early one morning before leaving for school to have a prayer with her and her mother. They were Catholics, and I didn't know a proper Catholic prayer, but in the midst of such a need, ecumenicity is no problem. We knelt, and I prayed for Kathy. Fear left the house, and she did improve for a while after that.

The day I was packing to move back to Kentucky, I heard Kathy shuffling across the yard as she hurried on her artificial leg to farewell me. She brought me a small Japanese doll in a glass case, smiling delightedly as she gave it to me. It was her farewell gift, and I still have it on my dresser today. Some months later, her lovely young life ended, but those of us who knew her will never forget how brave she was.

Maxine was another of my neighbors, a middle-aged mother with a serious heart condition. She stood between two generations. There was Rose, her lovely teenage daughter, and her elderly mother, now in her 90s. Caring for the mother alone would have taxed the strength of a well woman. Maxine often remarked that she knew God kept her alive because of her responsibilities to those two.

Every time I knocked on her door, she had time for a chat and a cup of tea. We spent many happy hours visiting together, both of us widows, with much to share.

Two years after I moved from the housing area, I learned that Maxine had died. Her daughter is now married; and the elderly mother, still clinging to life, is living with a family friend.

But during those days of intense study, I found I also needed some social life. I was bound to a daily discipline of study so rigorous that I had to rise at 6 a.m. on Sundays to prepare my Sunday school lesson. But on Saturday nights, I was lonely. I needed somewhere to go, a friend to talk with.

Then I found Myrtle, a charming woman in her mid-70s, slender and lovely, her once-red hair now gray. She bubbled with Irish wit. Myrtle could not drive, and being a widow was dependent on others to get around. Since I had learned to drive, we formed a mutual friendship. She entered into all my plans with great enthusiasm. She was ready for any adventure, as we drove the highways of southern Illinois in search of a different restaurant for our Saturday night dinners. One of our favorite spots was Ma Hale's Restaurant down in the Mississippi River country. Myrtle taught me that it is possible to form a deeply satisfying friendship with someone of another generation.

On my last visit with her this past spring, she was joyously packing for a trip to Hawaii with her sister. She was ecstatic as she thought about all the plans for the journey.

Some weeks following her return from Hawaii, she fell ill. In remembering her wonderful trip to Hawaii, she remarked one day that if her life didn't last much longer, she had no regrets for she had already been to Paradise once.

Since she was already 75, and owing to the serious nature of her illness, her friends and I prayed that her suffering would be shortened. It was only three more months before she went peacefully to that lasting Paradise. As I write these lines, I have just returned from her funeral in the small Illinois town where she lived. What a lovely friend she was!

How strange that all three of the special bridges I built during my two years in Illinois are all gone now, within four years of my leaving there. First of all, the youngest, then the middle-aged, and now finally the elderly friend—all gone. Perhaps God is saying to me, "Sylvia, keep on building more bridges."

One of the loveliest women I know is Lettie, who came to our college church more than two years ago to serve as our church visitor. During her first year of widowhood (her husband was a Methodist pastor) Lettie was given the assignment of visiting the shut-ins of our community, to comfort the sorrowing, and meet the needs of the hungry. And in this marvelous openhearted ministry to others, Lettie has found comfort in her own loss.

One exciting offshoot of Lettie's ministry is our Sunday school class for the single women of our church. In our large congregation with some 1,200 students in the pews on Sunday, it would be very easy for the single women of the church to feel somewhat lost. But thanks to Lettie, we are all alive and well. The women of our class come from all sorts of backgrounds and represent a wide age span.

On Sunday mornings we study the Word together around a large table and enjoy exciting discussions of various scripture passages. All of us look forward to Sunday school.

We enjoy potluck suppers, bowling parties, birthday parties, and attend various cultural programs in Lexington. We have made trips to historical places in our church bus, "Jerusalem."

When a woman lives alone, planning a vacation can be difficult. Last summer, four of our group shared a wonderful vacation at the beach. And two others made a flight together to California. Other class members met us upon return to the airport. Each has a desire to be a real "lifter-upper," not only to members of our group, but to others in the community. Thus we have chosen the name "Beacon Class." We hope to be a ray of light to any lonely person in the community whom we can contact.

On last July 4, our church congregation had a noon picnic at the old campgrounds. It was announced that we would eat in family groups. We women in our class formed our own "family" and enjoyed ourselves as we shared our picnic lunch together. There was no feeling of being a "fifth wheel" that day.

It has been said that if life shortchanges us in some way, there will be compensations if we will but look for them. To a casual onlooker, it may seem that my young son, Leland, was shortchanged in life with the loss of his father at age 11. Since Leland arrived so late in our family, he missed out on many of the exciting things that happened during our earlier years. Yet this very lack in his life has forced him to reach out to others and build bridges at a very early age.

After school hours, following his father's death, he visited at a neighbor's home until I came home from work. The father of that family was blind, which meant he was always at home. The family also had two sons older than Leland who shared in fun and games. The family members grew quite fond of Leland and he felt much at home with them. Because our own home nest was empty, he reached out and shared with other lives.

After becoming a teenager, Leland adopted the grandparents of another friend of his. Each Friday evening he still joins this friend to visit the grandparents for an evening of games. This elderly couple eagerly look forward to the boys' coming to their home to share an evening of fun with them. So Leland has surrogate grandparents. Having learned at such an early age to reach out and build human bridges, he will never know what it is to be lonely. What a wonderful compensation is his!

How exciting life can be as we learn from our Maker how to build bridges! What adventures we can experience as we enter into this creative, redemptive process. How tremendous to find ourselves in the mainstream of His great love, as we look out for others in need. We don't have all the answers for those in need, but as we build bridges, we can become the channels through which the Father can assuage the hunger and slake the thirst of other weary travelers on this globe.

9

The Furnace of Affliction

*The only people who have ever contributed sig-
nificantly to my life are people who have suffered,
and didn't let the suffering kill them. They let
the suffering draw them to Christ. And then they
became ministers of His grace, His compassion
and His love.*

—from a sermon by Dr. Dennis F. Kinlaw
President of Asbury College

I have often told my children, "If you can look up to
the Father and know that all is well between you and Him,
you can face anything." And in my lifetime I have had
ample opportunity to prove the truth of those words.

By faith, we can take Rom. 8:28 and make the prin-
ciple work in our lives. This great scriptural promise is
so beautifully paraphrased by C. H. Welch in his book
The Just and the Justifier, published by Leonard A. Can-
ning of Banstead, Surrey, England:

> The Lord may not have *definitely* planned that
> this should overtake me, but He has most certainly
> permitted it. Therefore, though it were *the* attack of
> an enemy, by the time it reaches me it has the Lord's

77

permission and therefore all is well. He will make it
work together with all of life's experiences for good
(p. 231).

Down in the subterranean depths of the soul, God
deals with each of us on His own terms. He has plans for
us, and as I grow older, I see that His plans are not made
for us alone. God's plans for His children overlap and
intertwine in a most remarkable way. That which affects
us as individuals carries vibrations along the complex
channel of human relationships. When God makes a certain move or change in our lives, the results are felt all
along this chain of interacting relationships, and often
in the lives of people unknown and unseen by us.

In the midst of trial we can "take our burden to the
Lord and leave it there." As we learn our lessons and draw
strength from Him, a strange and peculiar power will erupt
from our lives that will bring help and blessing to others.
All of this is none of our doing; it is simply His Holy Spirit
at work keeping the river flowing from within us. "The
secret of the Lord is with them that fear him" (Ps. 25:14).

As Christians, it is not only our privilege to win victory, but we can cry aloud with triumph right in the midst
of the bloody mire of spiritual battle. When I was a young
girl attending camp meeting, I used to hear some sister
testify: "Praise God! He gives me victory right in the face
of defeat!" I didn't fully comprehend the meaning of that
witness then, but now I know it well.

God knows, of course, just how much each of us can
endure, and He knows just what kind of test we can bear.
Some people are tender and brittle; they could easily be
crushed. They cannot stand too much pressure. Others
are so constituted that the harder you stomp on them, the
brighter they shine. But whatever our makeup, trouble
seems to come to all of us at one time or another.

A certain member of our women's Sunday school class

whose droll humor frequently sends us all into peals of laughter, remarked one day in class: "People have often commiserated with me about my family problems, and I have answered, 'Well, if it weren't that trouble, it would be something else. As long as you live in this world, you are going to have trouble, and if it isn't one kind, it will be another.'"

In Billy Graham's *Angels* the great drama taking place in earth's arena is well described:

> How would you live if you knew that you were being watched all the time . . . by the heavenly host? The Bible teaches in 1 Corinthians 4:9 that angels are watching us. Paul says we are a "spectacle" to them. . . . All true Christians participate in this great drama as they seek to obey Christ since this throws them into severe conflict with the forces of evil, who are bent on humiliating them (p. 157).

So it lies within the power of every Christian to enlist the power of the Holy Spirit to take the very plot Satan has devised to humiliate him and make that very scheme an instrument that will bring glory to God. The cross of Jesus was one such plot, cleverly devised to humiliate God's Son. But how proudly we Christians wear that emblem of our salvation!

Jesus told us, in fact, to expect trouble: "In the world ye shall have tribulation: but be of good cheer; I have overcome the world" (John 16:33).

Occasionally when treading deep waters, those words, "be of good cheer," have rung rather hollowly in my aching heart, because I didn't understand what He was really trying to tell me.

Many a Christian, in the crucible of affliction, having thrown himself into the comforting arms of the Father, has known, right in the midst of the trial, that joyous exaltation that comes from complete surrender to Him. Is there any bliss comparable to that exquisite joy God gives to His children when, by faith, they receive this gift of joy, while all around them is the turmoil of some earth-shaking trouble? I don't understand the workings of this divine joy, but I have experienced it in a very real way.

Sometimes in life we are called upon to witness from within the furnace. We can find strength for this kind of witnessing, for He enters the furnace with us, just as He entered the furnace with the three Hebrew children.

More than a quarter of a century ago when we were serving as young missionaries in South India, I was expecting our third child and had never been well during the entire pregnancy. The Swiss lady doctor in our community was very puzzled by my condition. I had grown to such a great size in so short a time. She finally concluded I had miscalculated my delivery date and sent me off to the mission hospital, a long day's journey by train, to await the coming of the baby. I was very puzzled, for I was sure the child was not yet full term. But obeying the doctor, I began my journey.

About halfway to the hospital, I stopped to rest overnight at the home of a dear missionary friend, Ruth. We had grown up together in the same small Illinois town, and had been as close as sisters since our late teens.

That afternoon, Ruth had invited a number of friends for afternoon tea, and among them was Rani Sahib, a widow of a member of India's ruling class. Rani wore ropes of real pearls and smoked little black cigars—a fascinating personality. She and Ruth were the only two women in that great city who could drive a car; Rani Sahib drove a flashy coupe with red leather upholstery, and my missionary friend drove a surplus army jeep.

Right in the middle of the tea party, as I sat hugely on one of the sofas trying not to be in the way, I suddenly became aware that labor pains had begun. As I glanced at

my watch, I realized I had just missed the train to Miraj
and the mission hospital, and it would be another four
hours before the next train would depart.

Rani Sahib, noting my glance at the watch and realizing something was amiss, took charge and drove me in
her car to a clinic down in the local bazaar where a Brahman lady doctor practiced obstetrics. She had her obstetri-
cal department upstairs in the clinic, while her husband (a
lung specialist) had his offices on the lower floor.

As the quiet, dignified Indian lady doctor examined
me, she softly said, "Mrs. Culver, I can't let you go on the
next train to Miraj. You would give birth on the train."
God knew I needed to be near my friend, Ruth, more than
I needed the aseptic cleanliness of the mission hospital.

Between trips home in the jeep to nurse her own new
baby, Ruth stood at my head, with her warm, comforting
hands on my forehead. (There was no time for my husband
to arrive until the next morning.) Identical twin boys were
delivered, premature as I had suspected, one dead at
birth and the other lived only a short time. We had no
incubator. They were fair—the very image of our second
son, Jon. Friends came forward to help prepare the tiny
coffin; and the babes were buried in a Christian cemetery
there in Belgaum, India.

The first few days following delivery, between feedings
of her own infant, Ruth drove the jeep over the rough, hilly
road to bring me food. I could never have subsisted on the
hot, spicy Indian diet. Because of an earlier injection with
an unsterile needle, a serious infection had set up in one
of Ruth's hips which was to plague her for the better part
of two years. At that time, the deep wound had been
cleansed and packed with bandages to keep it open and
draining. To drive the jeep over the rough roads was agonizing for her.

When she reached home one day, trembling in pain,

she prayed for God to send someone to help drive the jeep to bring food to me. Just at dusk, she heard a man's voice at her front door. Going to the door, she met a tall, young American. He needed a place to stay and had been sent to the mission bungalow. He was a Mormom entomologist, sent out to help the people of India find a way to prevent worms from forming in cashew nuts.

As soon as he made his need for lodging known, Ruth asked him, "Can you drive a jeep?" Upon being assured that he could, she invited him in. The same God who heard Hagar's weeping for her dying son, also heard the prayer of a young mother in pain, and in such a strange way sent an answer that could come only from Him. The tall young American drove her in the jeep daily to deliver my food.

During the first three days following the birth, I was unable to sleep. Deep sorrow, like an overwound mainspring, had become so deeply imbedded that I could not cry, and I could not sleep. It was my first brush with such sorrow, and I needed something extraordinary to help me through that dark hour. The doctors and nurses were very concerned. Having a foreign patient unexpectedly enter their clinic, and then to lose the babies, had been a great strain on them all.

It was just twilight on the third day, when I felt a Presence standing by my bed. No words were spoken, but I never felt such comfort. I knew Jesus was standing there, and He was greatly concerned for me. The terrible, dry tightness of grief began to gently unwind. I drifted off to slumber, even with all the noise of the hospital and the teeming bazaar around me. I knew nothing until morning.

My doctor's husband, a Hindu Brahman (the lung specialist) slipped upstairs the next morning and sat by my bedside. He gently inquired, "Mrs. Culver, tell me, how was it that after three days of no sleep, quite suddenly you were able to get sleep?" Then I told him of Jesus who came and stood by my bed. As long as I live, I shall never forget the thoughtful look in those deep brown eyes, and his attitude of profound respect as he listened to my story of Jesus, who came all the way to stand by the bedside of a sorrowing mother.

So God does not always choose to remove us from the furnace, but sometimes He gets down into the fire with us. Many times, just before some terrible catastrophe, I have heard how He has provided some word from the Bible, or some message from a friend to be a source of strength to help a Christian stand when all earthly props were removed.

God does not remove His children from this world with its pain and sorrow, but rather He comes to stand with them. He reaches out to us in our hour of pain and darkness and carries us through the crisis. Afterwards we come through the dark tunnel stronger and better than when we went in—and better equipped to serve Him. Something has been added—something greater than we ever knew before. This is His special gift to His children whom He loves so much.

I Will Guide Thee

I will instruct thee and teach thee in the way which thou shalt go: I will guide thee with mine eye (Ps. 32:8).

The outcome of a man's life is largely determined by his dreams and by his personal response to the guiding hand of a sovereign God. Young Joseph was such a dreamer; he dreamed that he would someday fill a high place and men would bow down to him. But Joseph was a prisoner before he became prime minister. Many years of struggle, heartbreaking delay, and discipline were to come before the fulfillment of his youthful dreams. But God's plan and purpose in his life moved right on, even in the face of slavery, unjust accusation, imprisonment, and delay.

In the Scriptures we find many exciting examples of the ways God led His children. And today, many Christians can bear witness of God's remarkable guidance in their lives. The longer we walk the Christian way, the more sensitive we become to His guiding hand. And often we must travel with sealed orders.

There is nothing that pleases Him more than the trusting faith of His children when everything seems to be going against His plan for their lives. Many times it is only "after the fact" that we begin to see the intricate pattern He has woven. We can see the exquisite detail of the design and the many obstacles swept aside which were right in the path of His sovereign will.

There are times when as we seek guidance in some situation, the Lord is leading us in a roundabout way. It seems as though we are walking through some strange maze. And then a door opens that He has had waiting for us all along.

In 1962, on our last furlough, we settled for a year in Glendale, Calif., while my husband was busy with deputational speaking tours. Since our youngest son was in kindergarten, I was unable to accompany him on his trips. Our second son, Jon, had just begun college so there was a real need for additional financial help. The solution, we felt, was for me to get a job.

For almost 10 years we had been gone from the States, and when I thought of the workaday world in the bustling metropolitan city around me, I really felt "out of it." I was like a foreigner in a strange land. I doubt that I had used the telephone more than a dozen times during our Taiwan years. I had, of course, maintained my secretarial skills, but the thought of trying to find a job in that strange city made me very uneasy. I scanned the newspaper for job openings, and began to pray. I didn't know how to begin to look for a job.

Some days later, I attended a PTA meeting in a nearby school where our youngest was enrolled. I kept noticing the young principal who conducted the meeting. I felt an urge to speak to him after the meeting, but I didn't know what I would say. Actually the meeting was rather boring and I was tempted to go home, but something restrained me. Finally, I thought, I'll ask him how to make application for a secretarial position in one of the Glendale schools.

After the meeting, I approached him and asked about making application for such a job. He answered in some detail, and then looking at me rather carefully, remarked, "You know, our church needs a secretary. Why don't you call our pastor?" He gave me the number.

Right away I telephoned the pastor of the church—a denomination other than my own—and went for an interview. But I had a problem: I could work only six hours a day. I had to be home when Leland came in from school.

The pastor later phoned me with regret, saying they really needed a full-time secretary. But he mentioned that the area office of their denomination, located a short distance from our home, often needed secretarial help. He suggested I call them.

Finding the large area office, I was welcomed by Mary, the redheaded supervisor of the secretarial pool, and the gentleman who served as personnel manager of the office. They really wanted a full-time girl but were so desperate to get experienced help in time to prepare for a forthcoming convention they took me on. I had a job! My wonderful boss, Mary, gave me a thorough grounding in office work and procedure.

Under Mary's expert guidance, I worked for a year with a dozen other girls in the secretarial pool. She saw to it that all of us rotated on the various assignments, thus broadening our skills. When she left for summer vacation, she put me in charge. I was thrilled to get such good work experience, and to enjoy the fellowship of Christian friends on the job. I did not know it then, but I was put in that particular job situation to prepare me to earn my own living when I would be left alone.

Sometimes, it happens that God uses us as instruments to meet special needs in the lives of others. My son,

Leland, had such an exciting experience during his senior year in high school.

One Sunday morning after service, he was walking through the church when he found lying on one of the pews a small cloth bag fastened with a safety pin. Opening the bag, he was astonished to find it full of a large roll of $20 bills. Excitedly, he carried the money to the pastor who later reported there was $900 in the bag. Leland was so excited he wanted to get on the phone and share his news with all his friends but his older brother and I restrained him. We suggested that if it were kept secret we could more easily find the real owner of the money.

On the following Saturday I had an appointment in the local beauty parlor. Geraldine, the owner of the shop, was cutting my hair. She began to tell a friend sitting in a nearby chair of her mother-in-law losing a large sum of money. She described the cloth bag and the safety pin. As I listened to her story, I nearly jumped out of the chair with excitement, but I kept quiet, because I felt the pastor should handle the matter. When she mentioned that they had been in church the previous Sunday, I knew I had found the one who had lost the money.

The following week the pastor took the bag of money to the happy lady who had lost it. She and Geraldine had both prayed that the money would be found. Geraldine later told me that she had told the story only that one time for fear word would get around that her mother-in-law carried such sums of money.

To show her joy and gratitude, the mother-in-law called Leland to her home and presented him with $100 as a reward. It was difficult to tell who was happier—the woman whose money was returned, or my son who found it.

At other times in our lives, God gives clear and definite guidance which at the time is not understood at all, but we recognize the "nudge" has come from Him and we step out completely on faith to obey His prompting.

A short while before moving to Illinois in 1970 to complete my college studies, I was lying in bed early one morning half awake when I got to thinking about my elderly father. He lived alone in a rather sleazy basement apartment in Herrin. During his latter years, Dad was very active in the local Senior Citizens Club where he spent his days in happy activity.

A strange urge came over me to call him by phone and invite him to make his home with Leland and me. But voices of fear echoed in my mind: "He is old. You are a widow and will have no salary. You plan to go to school. What will you do if he gets sick?" Yet somehow I knew in a moment that it was God who had brought this plan to my mind. Brushing aside my fears, I lifted the receiver, dialed his number, and the happy response at the other end of the line caused my heart to sing. I knew I was moving in the current of God's will.

But we needed housing—one of those miracles I had written on my list. Houses for rent were simply not to be had. Dad suggested we investigate the possibility of securing low-rent government housing. When we called on the man in charge at the rental office, we found out how important it was that I had invited Dad to live with us. Shuffling through his files, he remarked, "Mrs. Culver, you don't qualify for housing, since you have not been an Illinois resident. But your dad does qualify, and he has had an application in our files for two years." Imagine my feelings as I listened to his words! He promised us a three-bedroom duplex just as soon as there was a vacancy. Of course, at that time (February) there was no way of knowing just when such a vacancy would occur.

In June we moved to Illinois, put our furniture in storage, and took off for a month's visit with my oldest son in Hawaii. Just one week before we were due to return to Illinois a letter came from Dad: "I am all moved into the duplex. I am eating off a cardboard box. You had better get home and get your furniture out of storage."

So our house was waiting for us—and on time!

During the following spring, we had a bad ice storm. As my dad left the Senior Citizens Club that day on an errand, he slipped and fell on the ice. That evening he complained of a stiff shoulder and I remarked that it was fortunate he broke no bones.

All seemed well, but within a short time he began having headaches. He had never mentioned to me that he struck his head when he fell. Absorbed in my studies and grinding away at term papers and exams, I really didn't take enough notice of his headaches. Somehow I didn't connect them at all with his fall on the ice. Finally, one day friends brought him home from Senior Citizens Club, scarcely able to walk. I hurried him to the hospital emergency room.

I can still see him lying patiently on the table, his mind clear. He was able to answer all the routine questions asked of him. On the third night in the hospital, as he attempted to get up to the bathroom, he had another bad fall, striking his head hard on the floor.

That evening as I hurried into his room he had already begun to sink into a coma, but he smiled faintly up at me. (An autopsy later showed that the first fall on the ice caused a skull fracture that would at his age have taken him eventually. The second fall merely hastened his passing.) Since he was 79 years of age, the doctors gave us no encouragement. He never regained consciousness but passed away quietly a few mornings later just as he had lived, with little trouble to anyone.

For the second time within a few short years, it was my sad duty to dispose of the personal effects of a loved

one. But I could only feel a deep inner peace. When I made
the phone call that morning to invite Dad to live with us,
I did not know he had only seven more months to live. *But
God knew!* I was so grateful that he did not have to suffer
a long, lingering illness. I could only feel that God does all
things well.

On rare occasions when we are about to make an important decision, God uses unusual ways to get a message
through to us. In the spring of 1975, as I was making a job
change and felt the need of guidance, a strange letter came
from a man back in my home church in Illinois. John
Payne had prayed for us during our missionary years. He
had been healed of intestinal cancer some years earlier,
and because of all he had experienced, knew a great faith
in God. His letter read:

> I have been thinking and praying for you and have
> not heard anything about you. However, God tells me
> that you're standing on the brink of successes in your
> life that you have never had before. God is to pour out
> his blessing upon you that you cannot contain. Prepare
> yourself, the best you know how, to be in a position
> whereby the overflow will flood upon many people and
> that God will get the glory from your living.

Strange prophecy—strange source—strange timing.
I do not yet know the meaning of the letter, but how exciting to realize that God knows.

Always, in times of testing or decision, the Lord has
been my strength. He comes through with some word for
me. How rewarding when we are able to sit still and watch
Him fight our battles for us! So often I recall Uncle Bud
Robinson's famous sermon illustration: "When Satan gets
after me," he lisped, "I crawl down under the robes of
Jesus and peer out and say, 'Thick 'em, Jesus!'" How
beautiful!

It is comforting to know that His promise of guidance

is for all our lives. He has said, "Even to your old age I am he; and even to hoar hairs will I carry you: I have made, and I will bear; even I will carry, and will deliver you" (Isa. 46:4).

Sometimes at night with my head on my pillow, the question comes, "What next?" Then I reflect on the way God has led me these many years, and I can fall asleep—at peace. I know the same God who has led me thus far will not fail me now. Though the future is unseen and unknown to me—He knows it all.

And somewhere down the years ahead, there will come what people call "the end." But it will really be only the beginning of the greatest adventure of all. For, as Billy Graham puts it: "The way to life is by the valley of death, but the road is marked by victory all the way" (*Angels*, p. 152).